For Better & Better

For Better & Better

Building a Healthy Marriage for a Lifetime

Jeanette C. Lauer & Robert H. Lauer

DIMENSIONS
FOR LIVING
NASHVILLE

FOR BETTER AND BETTER:

Building a Healthy Marriage for a Lifetime

Copyright © 1995 by Dimensions for Living

This book is printed on acid-free, recycled paper.

Library of Congress Cataloging-in-Publication Data

Lauer, Jeanette C.
    For better and better : building a healthy marriage for a lifetime / by Jeanette C. Lauer and Robert H. Lauer.
        p.   cm.
    ISBN 0-687-23623-1 (acid-free paper)
        1. Marriage.   2. Interpersonal relations.   I. Lauer. Robert H.
    II. Title.
HQ734.L33615   1995
306.81—dc20
                                                                        94-12861
                                                                        CIP

Scripture quotations are from the New Revised Standard Version of the Bible, copyright © 1989 by the Division of Christian Education of the National Council of the Churches of Christ in the USA. Used by permission.

95 96 97 98 99 00 01 02 03 04 — 10 9 8 7 6 5 4 3 2 1

MANUFACTURED IN THE UNITED STATES OF AMERICA

To

those couples who have shared their marital journey with us

and

to those who have made our own journey immeasurably richer: Jon, Kathy, Julie, Jeffrey, Kate, Jeff, Krista, Benjamin, and David

Contents

1

*B*uilding a Healthy Marriage

*W*e once heard of a sad-eyed man who returned a book he had purchased. The book was entitled *Prayer Can Change Your Life*. "I'm sorry," he said, "I thought it said 'Prayer Can Change Your Wife.'" We have to give the man credit for wanting a better marriage. Unfortunately, he took a common but not helpful approach—everything will be all right if only my spouse changes.

So what is a helpful approach? How do you build a healthy marriage for a lifetime? A healthy marriage, incidentally, is not one that is trouble free, but one in which troubles are overcome. Challenges are confronted, problems are dealt with, and the partners remain committed through difficult times. At the same time, intimacy deepens, love grows, and the sense of oneness intensifies. In essence, a healthy marriage is both lasting and fulfilling.

Many marriages start out as satisfying but don't last. Others last but are not very satisfying. The partners stay together because of the children, economic realities, familial pressures, or religious beliefs. Or they stay married simply out of what we call relational inertia—the perpetuation of a boring, meaningless, or troubled marriage because neither partner takes the initiative to do anything about it.

In contrast, some couples create a lifelong adventure of love. We think, for example, of a couple we met in the Midwest. The last time we saw them they were in their nineties, married over sixty years. They still held hands and still looked at the world and each other with broad, contented smiles. They have both a lasting and a satisfying marriage—a model for all who want this kind of relationship.

They are one of hundreds of couples with whom we have worked in research, counseling, and marriage enrichment. We have interviewed more than 450 couples in long-term marriages to investigate the ingredients of healthy unions. We have seen what can go wrong and what can work well as we deal with couples in marital counseling. We have observed how couples grapple with issues and build intimacy in marriage enrichment groups. These experiences, combined with our own marriage of many years, convince us that couples can not only stay together, but can also find continuing romance and zest in their relationship. How? That's what this book is all about.

You Can Build a Healthy Marriage

A healthy marriage, like a healthy body, requires a periodic checkup. Your checkup covers nine resources that are crucial for a lasting and satisfying marriage: clearing away unrealistic expectations, commitment, compatibility, communication, coupling, conflict-management skills, change, community, and Christ. We begin our exploration of each resource with some "checkup" questions for you and your spouse. In each chapter, we also suggest a "prescription" to enhance or improve your relationship, along with some health-enhancing relationship exercises.

Clearly, building a healthy marriage requires effort and attention. But don't feel like you're being summoned to an exhausting and demanding task. The good news is that the effort and attention are often enjoyable. And the outcome—a lasting and satisfying marriage—is exhilarating!

2

*C*learing Away Unrealistic Expectations

"O that I might have my request, and that God would grant my desire."—Job 6:8

CLEARING AWAY CHECKUP

Answer each of the following questions, then read on to see how your expectations affect the health of your marriage.

1. What did you expect out of marriage that is not yet fulfilled?
2. How well does your spouse sense your needs?
3. In what ways do you expect your marriage to change?
4. Your spouse is responsible for your happiness. True or false?
5. In what ways would you like your spouse to be more like you are?

*E*xpectations are important. A high-achieving professional man told us about growing up with a father who repeatedly told him that he was stupid. "Looking back on it," he said, "I really did some rather senseless things. Like the time I forgot to turn off the gas burner under a heating tea kettle when my father called and had me run an errand. I narrowly missed burning down the house that time."

There is no way that you would label this man as senseless or stupid today. Yet he acknowledges that, as a boy, he did some stupid things. He also understands why: "It took me a lot of years to realize that I did some of those stupid things because my father expected me to act that way. Knowing what he thought of me made me too nervous to do things properly."

Expectations exist and are important in all relationships, including marriage. When the Hebrews married, they expected to have children. The biblical statement—"Now Sarai, Abram's wife, bore him no children" (Gen. 16:1)— was more than a casual comment. It was the announcement of a crisis that resulted from thwarted expectations. The crisis involved such things as Sarai's diminished sense of selfhood (Hebrew women were not considered to be fully human until they bore a son); Sarai's giving of her maid, Hagar, to Abram so that he might have children; and the subsequent conflict between Sarai and Hagar.

When expectations are unmet, relationships are likely to suffer. The problem is compounded by the fact that some expectations are voiced, and some are not. Some are realistic, and others are not. And those that are unvoiced or unrealistic, or both, can be deadly, as illustrated by the case of Jack and Kate.

Jack and Kate's marriage went well for the first year. Then it ran into Kate's expectations. Jack got angry with her one morning, called her "muddle-headed," and stormed out of the house to his place of work. When he got home that evening, calm and a little sheepish for what he knew was an overreaction, Kate had a surprise for him—she was ready to break up their marriage.

"I was devastated," she explained to a counselor. "It was like all the lights of hope went out in my life when Jack exploded. I actually thought about packing and leaving immediately, but I had to go to work myself. So I decided to tell him as soon as we both got home that either he or I would move out—that the marriage was over."

Was Kate also overreacting? It happens that this was Kate's second marriage. Her first had lasted only a short time, for she had unknowingly married a man who turned out to be verbally and, to some extent, physically abusive. Jack's anger that morning terrified her, because it reminded her of her first husband. And Kate had brought a very important expectation to this marriage, an expectation that she had not voiced to Jack but that the incident made clear. Her expectation was: "You will never act in any negative way that reminds me of my first husband and makes me wonder if you are like him."

Was Kate's expectation realistic? We think not. It was understandable in the light of her experience. Still, it was not realistic, and it could have wrecked her marriage if she and Jack had not sought help.

Unfortunately, this experience of Kate and Jack is not at all atypical. Unrealistic and unvoiced expectations trouble nearly all marriages to some extent. In many cases, they doom the relationship. In this chapter, we consider some of the more common but unrealistic expectations that people bring to marriage. Often people don't even realize they have the expectations. As we discuss each one, therefore, try to be candid about the extent to which you hold such an expectation. Then try our suggested ways to clear troubling expectations out of your marriage.

Unrealistic Expectation #1: You Will Fulfill All My Needs

"I, John, take thee, Mary, to be my lawfully wedded everything." No one makes such a vow at a wedding service. But if vows were based on expectations, some people would take the partner for a "lawfully wedded everything." For the idea that "you will fulfill all my needs" is one of the common unrealistic expectations that people bring to marriage.

Gracie, a young woman in premarital counseling, put it this way: "I think that my husband, rather than my family or friends, should be the one to fulfill all my needs for intimacy." She thought of it as a compliment to her fiancé. She was, after all, saying that she preferred him above all other people as an intimate companion.

But *all* her needs? What about her need for intimacy with God? What about her need for a circle of friends? What about her parents and siblings—would she really have no more need of their intimacy? What would happen when she ran into conflict in her marriage? Would she be completely without intimacy during that time? Gradually, as we discussed the matter, Gracie acknowledged that she was probably "starry-eyed" and expecting more than her husband-to-be could or even should deliver.

There's an old song entitled "You're My Everything." It sings of romance—an impossible and unhealthy variety of romance. God created Eve so that Adam would have "a helper as his partner" (Gen. 2:18). To expect a partner to be the source of all good in one's life is to cast the partner into the role of God rather than into the role of helper that God intended.

Permit your partner to be just what you are—a fallible human. Realize that each of you will find some of your needs fulfilled by others. This isn't a threat to your marriage. On the contrary, it liberates you from the burden of an impossible task. And that means an enhanced appreciation for the intimacy needs you fulfill in each other.

Unrealistic Expectation #2: You Will Sense My Needs When I Want You To

This unrealistic expectation is close to the first one, but not quite as encompassing. Rather, this expectation says: "There are times when I want you to do a specific thing or help me in a particular manner or respond to me in a certain way; and I want you to do it without me having to tell you."

This expectation is evident in the following exchanges, which we have heard time and again:

She: Sometimes at night I'm just exhausted. Why don't you pitch in and help with the house more?

He: Don't forget that I work all day, too. My job is as exhausting as yours. If you're especially tired some night, why don't you just ask me to help?

She: I shouldn't have to ask you. You can see how tired I am. You should just go ahead and do it.

\#

He: I wish we would make love more often.

She: I'm willing. But I get so busy I just forget about it sometimes. You need to let me know when you want to make love.

He: I don't want to always tell you. You should know that I need it without my having to tell you.

And so the battle of the sexes goes on over all kinds of issues. Once again, however, to want your spouse to be all-knowing—to know that you have a particular need at a particular time—is to cast your spouse into the role of God.

All things in marriage are a mutual responsibility. When you have a need, you have a responsibility to let your spouse know. Your spouse has the responsibility to respond. And vice versa. If you both understand and accept this responsibility, then you are each relieved of the burden of trying to be God. You no longer have to play guessing games with each other, and the quality of your relationship will improve measurably.

Unrealistic Expectation #3: Stay Just the Way You Are

"If Greta never changed a bit from the way she is now," Hank told us, "I would love her forever, and our marriage would be perfect." Hank was wrong. In the first place, Hank himself will change because change is inevitable. Will the new Hank still like the old Greta? For example, one of the things Hank now loves about Greta is "her spontaneity." What Hank calls spontaneity, some people would call being disorganized. Greta doesn't plan her life; she just goes with the flow. As they move along in their journey together and the demands of career and eventually, children, become overwhelming at times, will he still love Greta's "spontaneity"? Or will he prefer a Greta who is more organized?

Hank and Greta may one day illustrate one of the ironies of married life: that which first attracts you to someone may turn out later to be the source of trouble. In their case, "spontaneous" may turn into "irresponsible." In other cases, "He has a great sense of humor" became "He never takes anything seriously"; and "She is committed and loyal" became "She neglects me because she's obsessed with her career."

Keep in mind that it's often the same kind of behavior that is lauded at one point in time and is defined as intolerable at a later point. We change. We change in terms of what we like and what we need. So Hank is wrong. Even if it were possible for Greta to be exactly the same person ten years in the future, Hank would find himself reacting differently to her. And it's very likely that he would want her to change!

In the second place, change is the essence of a vital life. Happy people, noted the psalmist, are righteous people. "They are like trees planted by streams of water, which yield their fruit in its season" (Ps. 1:3). In other words, happy people are growing, changing people. Like trees, they develop and change as they mature. Would you plant a tree, and then try to suppress its growth? The real challenge to a Christian marriage is not to erect barriers to change, but to guide change so that you become more rather than less compatible over time.

Only God is changeless. Only God has no need to change. Both you and your spouse will, and will need to, change. Make your changes a cause for celebration by changing in ways that make you ever more attractive to each other. In contrast to Hank's statement, listen to that of a man married happily for three decades as he reflects with wit on the only wife he has had:

> I have been married to a series of women. They've all had the same name. And in some ways they're all alike. But each is different. My first wife was a housewife and mother. My second wife was actually a student. My third wife is a professional woman. And I like this last one best of all. She has all the good qualities of the other two, plus some new ones that they didn't have.

Change need not be a threat. When you change in ways that make you more compatible, change is a cause for celebration.

18

Unrealistic Expectation #4: You Are Supposed to Make Me Happy

Well, yes and no. "Yes," if you both agree that you have a mutual responsibility to contribute to the happiness of the other. But "no," if whether you make me happy is the test of our marriage. One of the factors at work in the million plus divorces each year is the notion: "If it were not for you, I would be happy."

Of course, it is not our goal to be unhappy. The point is that marital happiness is a matter of what "*we* need to do," not just what "*you* need to do." We have observed with troubled couples that each spouse can answer the question: "What can *your spouse* do to improve this situation?" Invariably, the unhappy husband or wife is somewhat startled, and gropes for words, when we pose the question: "And what can *you* do to improve the situation?"

It's fascinating what can happen when each partner accepts responsibility for marital happiness. Just knowing that your spouse is concerned about your happiness gives you a boost. And when you each start acting on your responsibility, your relationship will begin to flourish.

Mark and Donna took action after eight somewhat turbulent years of marriage and three children. Each faulted the other for failing to "make me happy." Neither wanted divorce, though each had toyed with the idea and each questioned whether they could ever survive together. The situation improved dramatically (though not without setbacks) when they stopped faulting and started problem solving. They drew up individual lists of things to do to help the other and began doing them. For the first time in eight years they began addressing the question: "What can I do to improve my marriage?" In asking the question and finding the answers, they created a strong marriage.

Unrealistic Expectation #5: You Should Be More Like Me

"If things were ideal," we once heard a husband say, "we would each always want the same things at the same time in the same amount. Then we would never argue about anything." It is true that a good deal of marital conflict arises because a husband and wife differ. For example, one is a saver, and the other is a spender. One wants sex three times a week, and the other is content with less. One likes to be up early, the other prefers to sleep in. One wants everything organized, the other likes to go with the flow. One wants to talk everything out, the other would rather forget what has happened and move on.

Some differences are inevitable in any marriage. The problem is not so much the differences as the attitude "you should be more like me," which often means: "the way I do it is the right way, and yours is the wrong way." Yet it isn't a matter of right and wrong. It's a matter of personality differences or individual preferences.

For example, Carl and Jane are a young couple struggling to maintain their marriage of three years. Carl is a sales manager. He is a highly organized individual and wants his home to be equally organized. Jane, on the other hand, works part-time as a teacher's aide and loves to spend as much time as possible with their four-year-old son and their two dogs. "For me, there's no contest when it's a choice between straightening up the house," she admits, "and going for a walk with our dogs or taking our son to the playground. The house just isn't that important to me."

What Carl and Jane had to recognize was that they were dealing with preferences rather than right and wrong. For Carl, "I prefer living in an ordered home" came out as "Jane isn't fulfilling her responsibility to keep the house clean."

For Jane, "I prefer to maximize my time with our child and pets" came out as "Carl actually believes a clean house is more important than doing things with our son or taking care of the dogs."

Carl and Jane are still working on the issue. However, they have a big advantage now. They at least recognize that they are dealing with preferences rather than sins. They have each moved from "you should be more like me" to "I understand your preference and you understand mine, so how can we deal with this in a way that's acceptable to each of us?"

Clearing away unrealistic expectations is important for the health of your marriage. Keep in mind that when you clear away the unrealistic expectations, you are building healthy ones at the same time. The following suggestions will help you to identify those that are unrealistic and to change them or get rid of them.

RX FOR COUPLES: CLEAR AWAY UNREALISTIC EXPECTATIONS

1. Draw up separate lists of your expectations.
2. Discuss the lists together.
3. Work together to make *necessary* changes.
4. Repeat the procedure as needed.

Read on for more explanation.

1. Draw up separate lists of your expectations. We suggest that you and your spouse each think about your expectations in a number of areas and write them down on separate lists. Among other things, you will want to think carefully about what you expect in a variety of key areas: the role of husband; the role of wife; the role of parent; our interaction with the extended family; the way the family spends money; the way we handle conflict; our sexual relationship; communication; time management, including how to spend leisure time and the amount of time spent together and separately; and household division of labor.

You may want to add some areas that reflect your personal situation. There are two ways to identify such areas. First, if you ever say or think to yourself "I just don't know what you want" or "You just don't understand what I want," you are probably dealing with an expectation that needs to be clarified and addressed. Second, think about the things that are the most common sources of conflict; some of them may involve unarticulated and unmet expectations.

2. *Discuss the lists together.* Begin with one area, such as the role of husband. You and your spouse begin by reading each other's list of expectations. Note any disparities, any contradictions, and discuss how you can come to agreement.

For instance, Carl and Jane, whom we spoke of earlier, had differing ideas about the role of husband. Jane's list of expectations began with "show affection in some way every day." Carl's list didn't include that. It began with "bringing home the bacon." Carl thought a husband's primary responsibility is providing the material necessities of life; Jane thought a husband's primary responsibility is providing the emotional needs of his wife. They agreed that the health of their marriage depended on discussing and working out some kind of resolution to the difference.

3. *Work together to make necessary changes.* "Necessary" means that not every difference needs to be worked out.

22

Some differences may be trivial or unimportant to you. If Carl's expectation that a husband's primary duty is to provide materially for his wife had not affected the quality of his marriage, he and Jane could have shrugged it off and given their attention to more critical areas. Part of your discussion is deciding which expectations point to a need for change.

In Carl and Jane's case, they both agreed that their understanding of the husband's role required change. Comparing their lists was a revelation for each of them, for each had misinterpreted the other. Jane had felt that Carl's preoccupation with work meant a loss of interest in her. Carl had assumed that material success was necessary to maintain her respect and love.

The knowledge that Jane valued him more for who he was rather than for what he accomplished at work was liberating for Carl. However, he also experienced some anxiety because he initially interpreted Jane's statement as desiring more frequent sexual relations and extended personal attention. He wasn't certain that he had either the time or the energy to comply. Actually, Jane would have liked both. However, through their discussions they worked out a workable solution: a daily kiss and embrace and discussion of the day's happenings at a minimum, and more when Carl's energy level permitted.

Don't be misled by the relative ease with which Carl and Jane worked through this issue. Many changes will not be easy. The procedure is not a painless way to bring more harmony to your marriage. It is a way to identify—in order to deal with—the unmet, the unarticulated, and the unrealistic expectations that detract from the quality of your marriage. And that is likely to require a good deal of thought and energy and patience. In chapter 8, we'll give you some additional help in bringing about changes in each other.

4. *Repeat the procedure as needed.* When do you need to repeat the procedure? An obvious time is when you sense that your marriage is troubled or is no longer fulfilling. But we would recommend more than the obvious—a periodic checkup of your mutual expectations about your life together. Why? Because expectations change. They are transformed by time, experience, and external stimuli—friends, family, television, movies, books, and magazines. Any of these can create new expectations about yourself and your marriage that can cause difficulties if they are not acknowledged and accommodated in a satisfactory way.

EXERCISING CLEARING AWAY

Do the following as a couple or in a group with other couples.

1. With your spouse, develop the "ten commandments of unhealthy expectations." Have each commandment begin with "We should not expect each other to. . . ."
2. Similarly, develop the "ten commandments of healthy expectations" with each one beginning with "We should expect each other to. . . ."
3. Each of you list your marital short-term and long-range goals and then compare these lists to determine where your expectations agree and disagree.

3

Commitment

Set me as a seal upon your heart.
—Song of Solomon 8:6

COMMITMENT CHECKUP

Answer each of the following questions, then read on to see how commitment affects the health of your marriage.

1. On a scale of one ("I frequently have thought about divorce") to five ("I would do anything to make this marriage work"), how would you rate your commitment to your spouse?
2. How would you rate your spouse's commitment to you on the same scale?
3. How has your commitment grown or diminished during your marriage?
4. What would happen in your marriage if you and your spouse's commitment to each other deepened?

Rumor has it that many people today shudder at the very mention of the "C" word—*commitment.* We think there is some substance to the rumor. A young woman bluntly told us why she is reluctant to make a commitment: "In a world where there are so many things to do and see, how can you commit yourself to a relationship which will, in effect, most likely hinder your opportunities for experience and growth?"

The tragedy of such a perspective lies in its blindness to the "opportunities for experience and growth" that can only come through commitment. Without commitment there is no intimacy. God has shown us this; the biblical message is that God "will not fail you or forsake you" (Deut. 31:6) when you are in an intimate relationship with him. In other words, God has committed himself to us, assuring us that we can count on him, and reminding us in the process that commitment is the only way to true and full intimacy.

What Is Commitment?

What exactly is this commitment that is so essential to a lasting and satisfying intimate relationship? In essence, commitment to another person is the promise to be faithful in the task of bonding. To say to someone, "I commit to you," is to say, "I promise to devote myself to the work of bonding with you, and I promise to work with you to allow nothing to intrude into or to sever the bonds that we shall form."

God has not only demonstrated the necessity, but also the meaning, of commitment: "I have loved you with an everlasting love; therefore I have continued my faithfulness to you" (Jer. 31:3). God has promised to devote himself to the work of bonding with us.

Commitment to someone, then, is not a grim surrender to stay with another person no matter how miserable you both are. It is a shared pledge to build a fulfilling relationship. It is a way of saying to the other person: "You can count on me to remain with you. I won't leave you just because we're having problems, or because you don't measure up to all I had hoped. You can count on me to work with you to overcome all those issues and to construct a marriage that will be enriching to both of us."

To What Should You Commit Yourself ?

The commitment that helps fashion a lasting and satisfying Christian marriage involves your partner, but it involves more. In fact, the commitment is threefold, and each of the three features is a vital part of your marriage.

1. Commit yourself to Christ. A shared faith adds glue to a marital relationship. We like to ask engaged couples, "What do you see as some of the strengths of your relationship?" A young woman said, "I think religion is one of our strengths, but you probably won't like the reason." Puzzled, we told her to continue. "It's a strength," she said, "because neither of us is very religious. So religion isn't a divisive factor in our relationship."

Knowing they had planned a church wedding, we pursued the matter with them: "May we ask, then, why you want to be married by a minister in a church?" Each struggled to give an answer to the question, using such terms as *tradition* and *appropriate.* The young man, we noticed, was uneasy. He had been raised in a Christian home and had been very active in church until his late teenage years. In a hesitant, somewhat rambling response, he tried to leave the door open to future spiritual growth and involvement in church. Clearly, he was not as comfortable as his fiancée with the notion of being nonreligious.

In a sense, the young woman was right. Shared values strengthen a relationship, and they shared the value that religion is unimportant. But in another sense she was wrong. Her fiancé seemed to be heading in a different direction than she was. He obviously wanted to keep open the possibility of once again being active in church. Thus, the strength of this shared value was precarious at best.

Even if they gained a certain strength from their present shared indifference to religion, they would miss the bonding power of a shared faith. Consider what it means when two people are committed to Christ, meet each other, fall in love, and get married. A Christian man, married for twenty-two years, expressed it well: "I believe that God brought us together. I believe that God will help us stay together. And I believe that God will make our life together a rich and joyous experience." In other words, a shared faith adds glue to marriage because your coming together in the first place is not mere chance but is one of God's creative acts. Moreover, all the resources of the God who brings you together are available as you construct a lasting and meaningful marriage. Commitment to Christ, then, is the bedrock upon which your marital union can remain firm.

2. Commit yourself to marriage. We don't mean merely to agree to get married, as in "marry, don't just live together." We mean something more. As one committed to Christ, you are committed to his teachings. And that means, among other things, to honor marriage as a sacred institution—to really understand marriage as a "holy state."

Just as with anything else that is holy to God, marriage must be treated with reverence. It is not like an old coat, to be casually discarded when it no longer pleases. Ministers who point out in a wedding service that marriage is "not to be entered into lightly" are reminding their hearers that God takes marriage seriously.

What are the consequences of regarding marriage itself (not just your own marriage) as that which is holy to God? "I feel locked in," a young married woman told us. "But in a good sense—I feel secure. I know that neither my husband

28

nor I would ever think of breaking up. Our marriage is God's calling."

"Locked in." Contrast that with a young bride who wrote her own marriage vows. Instead of "till death us do part," she and the groom pledged themselves to the union "as long as we love each other." (We are happy to report that a justice of the peace, not clergy, performed the ceremony.)

In other words, if marriage is sacred, then your union is God's call as well as God's blessing. You would no more think of breaking it up because of problems or because your ardor for your mate has cooled for a time than you would think of having a picnic in a church sanctuary. To be committed to the institution of marriage as a sacred covenant is to add a great deal of stability to your own marriage.

3. *Commit yourself to your spouse.* Like our commitment to Christ, commitment to a spouse is meant to be without contingencies. "As long as we don't argue," "as long as you treat me the way I want," "as long as I find you attractive," "as long as we still think we love each other" are not part of the initial covenant. In one way, however, commitment to spouse differs radically from commitment to Christ. For Christ does not break his commitment to us. But your spouse may break faith with you. The question is, do you stay committed to someone who no longer has a commitment to you? Do you stay committed to a relationship that is meaningless or stressful or even destructive?

We believe you should consider a number of things if you are in a situation where such questions arise. First, keep in mind that many counselors agree that most marriages that end in divorce could have been saved. Most importantly, they could have become good marriages. The assumption underlying many divorces is: "If I were married to someone else, I wouldn't be having these problems." This assumption is usually false. All married couples have problems. With a different mate, you might have the same problems or some different ones. But you will still have problems.

Second, you can work through most problems and, in the process, your marriage will become stronger. You may need to hone your skills at handling conflict (see chapters 5 and 7). You will certainly need to draw upon your faith. You may even need counseling at some point. However, there are abundant resources from God, from other people, and from within yourself that you can use to confront and overcome the problems of marriage. It is reassuring to know that people have dealt successfully with every kind of disruptive problem from lack of communication to marital infidelity.

Third, there is a kind of commitment that we view as inadequate and even destructive: "We stay together for the sake of the children." We shudder when we hear someone say that. For it frequently means either a highly conflicted relationship, a cold war, or a loveless marriage in which the spouses are uninvolved with each other. In any case, the effects on the children may be worse than if the couple divorced.

A man we have known since his childhood has spent many hours of his adult life in a psychiatrist's office. A major part of his problem was the home in which he grew up. His parents stayed together, but it was a home without love. "I never saw my mother and father show any kind of affection toward each other," he told us. "They didn't fight. But neither did they have much to do with each other. They lived together like strangers." And the impact on their two children was grievous. Neither have married. Both continue to struggle with emotional problems.

We do not believe that God calls people to stay together for the sake of the children when the impact on the children is destructive. God calls couples, rather, to work out their problems and build a strong relationship. One of the worst things you can do to children is to force them to live in a home where there is a miserable marriage. But one of the best gifts you can give your children is a stable and satisfying marriage.

Fourth, what do you do if you are true to your commitment but your spouse is not? Sometimes a spouse refuses to accept any responsibility for marital problems: "I don't need to go to a marriage counselor; you're the one who needs to change." Sometimes a spouse even denies that there are problems.

Tom had been married five years when he asked us for help. His wife told him she no longer loved him. She found some of his habits offensive (he wore outdated clothes), and some of his behavior exasperating (he had been depressed about his job situation). Tom was still committed, but perplexed about what he could do in the situation:

> She won't agree to counseling, because she says it's too late. If I tell her I'll try to change, she says it won't make any difference. If I tell her I still love her, she says she's sorry but she can't love me. If I tell her a divorce will be hard on our daughter, she says she's sorry but it would be harder if we stayed together.

At first, Tom's situation seems hopeless. It takes two people to make a marriage, and two to remake it when it has faltered. Or does it? In the long run, yes. In the short run, there is something that the committed partner can do even without any cooperation from the spouse—namely, change the pattern. When a marital relationship is deteriorating, one partner may try to repair it by redoubling efforts that failed earlier. For example, when Tom's wife first told him that their marriage was dead, he assured her of his love. That didn't change things, so he began to tell her more frequently that he loved her. The pattern they were in was one in which she kept telling him that the marriage was over while he redoubled his efforts to convince her it could still work. It seemed a reasonable thing for Tom to do, but it didn't make a dent in his wife's determination to end the relationship.

We told him to change the pattern. That meant to stop pouring out reasons why the marriage could survive. It also meant to direct Tom's energies into something different. One possibility, we suggested, was to focus on his daughter and on his work. "Act as if you're going to be single again," we said. "Strengthen your relationship with your daughter and get yourself into the best possible condition spiritually, physically, and emotionally." For example, Tom told us that he had offered to go to church regularly with his wife if she would try to save their marriage. We told him not to wait for her but, instead, to go by himself and get the spiritual nourishment he so desperately needed.

We told Tom one other thing:

If you do such things, if you change the pattern of your life and the relationship with your wife, she might begin to respond to you. However, she might not. But in either case, you will have served yourself and your daughter well. Moreover, it's your only option. You clearly can't change your wife right now, but you can change yourself. If it saves your marriage, great. If not, you will be able to handle the divorce far better than you can right now.

Tom began to change the pattern. It was difficult, especially at first when he desperately wanted to persuade his wife to work on their relationship. Gradually, Tom began to feel better about himself. Through the church, he got spiritually anchored. He began to function better at work. He spent more time with his daughter and delighted in her. His wife took notice. She began to see a Tom who was once again attractive. They are now working together on their relationship. We think they'll make it.

Finally, even though your commitment to your spouse is without contingencies, that does not mean that it binds you irrevocably together. "Without contingencies" means that you enter marriage with the full intent to confront and overcome every difficulty, every problem, and build a lasting and satisfying union. It does not mean that you stay with someone regardless of what that person does to you or your relationship.

When we commit ourselves to Christ, we commit to one who will never abuse, never break faith, never betray, but who will always love and cherish. However, humans don't measure up to such standards. Thus, Jesus said that adultery breaks the marital covenant (Matt. 19:9). Adultery breaks the covenant because it is a direct assault upon, and rejection of, the biblical call to "one flesh."

Similarly, we believe that an abusive relationship is a direct assault upon and rejection of the call to "love your wives, just as Christ loved the church" (Eph. 5:25). We have known women who stayed in an abusive relationship for years—to their own and their children's detriment—because ministers and family members urged them to be true to their commitment. We do not believe that God calls anyone to enter into or to stay in an intimate relationship with someone who is destructively abusive.

Abusers rarely, if ever, stop their abusive behavior without professional help and a spiritual transformation. Unfortunately, they are unlikely to get help or to experience transformation, because they rarely recognize the problem as their own. It's always "you made me do it." In the case of abuse, then, there is no covenant relationship to which to commit, for the abuser has assaulted and rejected the call to love as Christ has loved.

Why Should You Strengthen Your Commitment?

Commitment enriches marriage in a number of ways. First, it gives you a base upon which you can work through difficulties. After all, why go through the hassle of working out problems unless you can count on the relationship lasting? If the commitment of one or both partners is weak or questionable, there is little motivation to tough out the more trying days or to put the necessary energy into enhancing the quality of your marriage.

Second, commitment nurtures security. To know that your spouse is committed to you is to have some emotional security in a turbulent world. A wife told us of her husband's commitment: "I always feel that he's there if I need him. Security is important. He's dependable. I can count on him more than anybody else I know."

Third, commitment assures you of support. Stress comes to every life, but the effects of stress are minimized when you have supportive relationships. Support, in other words, is good for your health. And knowing that someone is committed to you assures you of such support. A man happily married for thirty-five years told us: "To know that you have someone to love you, someone you can depend on no matter what problems may arise is really important.

It's like having a cast on a broken leg that you can rely on to support you."

———

We tend to think in "either-or" terms. Someone is either committed or not committed. However, commitment is an ongoing process; it grows and develops with time, experience, and even practice. You and your partner can practice strengthening your commitment to each other.

RX FOR COUPLES: STRENGTHEN YOUR COMMITMENT

1. Tell your partner about your commitment and your commitment concerns.
2. Practice self-instruction.
3. Use marital team-building techniques.
   Read on for more explanation.

1. Tell your partner about your commitment and your commitment concerns. Like the patient who doesn't want to tell the doctor about his symptoms because he fears the diagnosis, couples sometimes are reluctant to raise the issue of commitment because they fear the response. But that only feeds and perpetuates whatever anxieties they have. As Frank and Brenda, a young couple married six years, discovered, it's better to be open about the matter. Brenda's job requires her to travel a lot. Before a recent trip, she and Frank argued strenuously over some budget matters. Brenda left with the conflict unresolved. Frank calmed down by the next day, and felt badly about the fact that they had parted with animosity between them. He would call her, he thought as he shaved. He cut himself, and looked for some first-aid cream. He suddenly realized that Brenda's birth control device was not in the drawer where she usually kept it. Then he remembered that this was the trip where she would meet a good friend—a male friend who was also a business associate.

Fear gripped him. Would Brenda, in her anger, betray him? Had she taken the birth control device with her accidentally or purposely? For the rest of that day, Frank agonized. Finally, he called Brenda. He recalls the conversation going something like this.

"I feel like a fool even asking this, but it's really tearing me up. Why did you take your diaphragm with you?"

"What are you talking about?"

"I was looking for first-aid cream, and noticed it wasn't here."

Brenda told him to wait a minute. When she returned to the telephone she said, "It's in my bag. I guess I just threw it in with my other stuff because I was rushing."

"I thought, I was afraid, I mean. . . ," he faltered.

"Look," she interrupted him, realizing what he was struggling to say, "I'm sorry we fought before I left. But that's one thing you never have to worry about. I would never cheat on you."

When Brenda returned home, she and Frank worked up a schedule that would allow them to spend more time together nurturing their marriage. Openly talking about their commitment led them to take steps to deepen it.

2. *Practice self-instruction.* Self-instruction is useful for managing many kinds of behavior. If you've ever resisted temptation by saying to yourself, "Don't do this, you'll hate yourself in the morning," you were using self-instruction. In the case of marriage, self-instruction is helpful when you

are feeling indifferent or troubled or frustrated or angry with your spouse. The self-instruction might go something like this: "Hang in there, because you'll be far happier in the long run. Every marriage has problems; this is one of those times you have to endure."

Self-instruction is not a substitute for dealing with problems. Keep in mind that commitment includes a willingness to confront and work through problems. But during those vexing days while working on a problem, self-instruction can deepen your commitment and help you avoid the temptation either to give up or to try to ignore the problem.

A young housewife told us how she uses self-instruction:

> I once read that arguments can actually be good for your marriage. I hate them. But when we have one, I remind myself that my marriage is going to be better because we're having this awful argument. If I didn't tell myself that, I'd probably just give in to get it over with. And I know that's not good.

3. Use marital team-building techniques. Team building is widely used in business to increase the solidarity of work groups. A common team-building technique is to engage in activities based on shared goals. One of the outcomes of a team-building activity is greater commitment to the group on the part of the members. Marital team building is based on the same premise—that pursuing shared goals increases your commitment to each other. We would like to suggest three things you can do to engage in marital team building.

First, use the following team-building exercise. You and your spouse should each write down your goals and the goals you believe are held by the other. Include goals in various areas of your life, such as church involvement, work or career, family, leisure activities, major purchases, and vacations. Then share your lists and discuss your answers. You should now more fully understand the goals that each of you has, and you can work together to create more common goals.

Second, watch your language. To what extent do you use "I" and "my" versus "we" and "our"? Too much "we" may signal an unhealthy dependence. But too much "I" may signal a deficiency in shared goals. For example, how do you handle your finances? Many couples decide to have three accounts—his, hers, and ours. Since money is a common source of conflict, you have to work out your finances in a way that is comfortable for both of you. But we recommend that you try a single account, and that your budget have a small discretionary fund for each of you. You can each spend your discretionary fund in any way you please. No questions are asked. All the rest is "ours" rather than "mine" or "yours." Couples with long-term, satisfying marriages maximize the amount of "ours" in their relationship.

Third, always maintain a certain amount of "marriage time." Time spent with children, parents, and friends is necessary and good. But it is not marriage time. No matter how many demands you face—from work, family, friends, and organizations—you need to plan shared activities that involve just the two of you.

A friend who has a "great marriage" told us that at one point his marriage was "going down the tubes." Ironically, it was happening, he said, "because of people and things we loved." Various activities with friends and family consumed so much time and energy that they had virtually no marriage time.

By definition, team building means spending time together. It's the only way to build commitment. Remember, no matter how busy you are, you can always come up with additional ways to increase your time together. For example, one couple decided to change the way they did their household chores. Instead of "you do this while I do that," they decided to do most things together. That way, they could talk together even though they were working.

The child-rearing years are probably the most difficult ones in which to find marriage time. During these years, it is, of course, vital that you spend time together as a family. However, it is equally important that you continue to nurture your marriage. And if you feel guilty about time spent as a couple, keep this in mind—one of the best things you can do for your children is to give them a vital and happy relationship between you and your spouse. Every counselor knows the amount of emotional wreckage among people who didn't have that gift. Marriage time isn't selfishness. It's time spent preparing a precious gift that will enrich you, your family, and your world.

EXERCISING COMMITMENT

Do the following as a couple or in a group with other couples:

1. Each of you complete the sentence: "I would feel more committed to you if I. . . ." Share and discuss your answers.
2. Repeat the above with the sentence: "I would feel you are more committed to me if you. . . ."
3. Establish a daily "couple time" (no matter how brief) for sharing and cuddling.
4. Write out three to five self-instructions that can support commitment during troubling times. Use as needed.

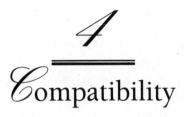

Compatibility

A friend loves at all times.
—Proverbs 17:17

COMPATIBILITY CHECKUP

Answer each of the following questions, then read on to see how compatibility affects the health of your marriage.

1. In what areas of your life do you feel most compatible with your spouse?
2. In what areas do you feel least compatible?
3. How have you grown more, or less, compatible since you were married?
4. To what extent is your spouse your best friend?
5. How often do you and your spouse laugh together?

hat is compatibility? It must be important, because most people agree that you're not likely to have a stable and happy marriage without it. Yet despite its importance, most people also have inadequate notions about what compatibility is.

What Does Compatibility Mean?

When discussing with couples during premarital counseling what attracted them to each other, virtually all agree that they have a high degree of compatibility. "We're very compatible" is a common response to the question "What do you like about each other?" When asked to be specific, the couples talk about various ways in which they form a harmonious unit: their personalities work well together; they enjoy the same leisure activities; they have similar values; their partners have qualities that nicely complement their own; and so on.

That, indeed, is what compatibility is all about—two people who have qualities and habits and values and goals that make them a harmonious unit. "Opposites attract" is a well-known saying. It's true for magnets. It isn't true for people. The more alike two people are, the more they are attracted to each other because it is the likeness that makes for compatibility.

People who are alike in such basic matters as values and aspirations may be powerfully attracted to each other even in the face of other factors that would separate them. Rick and Fran, a young couple married for three years, are a good illustration. Rick is African American and Fran is white. They met at church and were immediately attracted to each other. Although Fran knew that her parents would strongly resist her dating a black man, she began to go out with Rick. As she expected, their relationship developed in the face of strong opposition from Fran's parents as well as from some of her friends, who asked her if she realized the consequences of a mixed marriage.

When the couple decided to marry, Fran's parents said they would not attend the wedding. Fran had always been close to her parents. Their decision hurt her deeply. But she would not back down despite their opposition. Fran explained why: "Except for race, Rick and I are so much alike. We are committed Christians. We like to do things together, and we have fun together. We have the same goals in life. I like the kind of person he is, and I know he likes the kind of person I am. I know it sounds corny, but this is a marriage made in heaven."

Fran's parents are finally becoming reconciled to the union. "They see how happy we are together," she pointed out. Their prejudice has, of course, been bitter for Rick. "But he's a very forgiving person. I have a lot of hope for the future."

Compatibility—and that means being alike—adds a lot of glue to a relationship. To say that compatibility involves being like someone else does not mean that there are no differences. Compatibility is also fostered by different traits that complement each other. For instance, one way in which Rick and Fran are different is that she's an extrovert and he's an introvert. It works out well for both of them. At parties, Fran carries the conversation along, and Rick enjoys the group without having to feel responsible for keeping things going.

But a word of caution. Rick is only slightly introverted, and Fran is not a strong extrovert. A marriage between a strong extrovert, with a high need for mingling with people, and a strong introvert, with a high need for substantial amounts of private time, could involve serious problems. For instance, such a couple could engage in an ongoing tug-of-war over how much time to spend in social activities and how much time to spend at home.

When differing qualities complement each other, however, they can enhance compatibility. Nevertheless, it is the similarities between people that are the bedrock of a compatible union.

Compatibility Is a Process

Think for a moment about all the couples planning to get married who rejoice in their compatibility. Sadly, one can't help thinking about the fact that many of these couples will find themselves in divorce court some day. So what happens to their compatibility? They lose it. They don't realize, or they forget, that compatibility is not just something you have; but rather it is something that you must work to maintain and even to build. Compatibility is a process rather than a state.

How can that be? Aren't you either alike or not alike? Yes and no. As we noted, most partners believe that they are alike when they begin their intimate journey. Yet the fact that you are alike now doesn't mean you will stay that way. And the fact that you have certain differences now that are vexing does not mean that these will always mar the quality of your marriage. Everyone changes over time. The challenge to a satisfying marriage is for each partner to change in a way that enhances rather than diminishes their compatibility.

Consider Meg, who is studying to be a teacher. Meg married soon after graduating from high school. At the beginning of her marriage she envisioned being a housewife and mother. After ten years of marriage and two children, Meg decided she wanted to prepare for a new career. The decision could have caused problems in her marriage, as it has for some women. She told us:

I have friends who decided to do the same thing I did. We loved being wives and mothers, but those responsibilities were taking less and less of our time, and we needed a new challenge. My husband was very supportive. He encouraged me to pursue a graduate degree and helped me around the house so that I could take classes at the university. But some of my friends weren't so fortunate. When they embarked on a different career, they started having marital problems. Their husbands resented what they were doing.

But in Meg's case, both she and her husband changed in a way that maintained and even enhanced their compatibility.

One thing that helped Meg and her husband remain compatible was that they discussed her developing aspirations. They talked about her feelings of frustration and her need for new challenges. Together they explored her options. Long before she actually enrolled in classes, they discussed the ways in which her return to school would affect their family and marriage. In other words, it was a shared adventure. Keeping in close touch with each other's changing perspectives is an important part of staying compatible.

Another important aspect to nurturing your compatibility is based on the fact that being compatible means that you are alike, that you enjoy doing the same kinds of things, and that it's basically fun to be with your partner. In other words, the ingredients of compatibility sound much like the elements necessary in a solid friendship. This is a point we need to consider carefully.

Who Is Your Best Friend?

Who in the Bible provide a good example of a strong friendship? When we ask people this question, the answer is usually David and Jonathan. How about Abraham and

Sarah? Or Peter and his wife? The answer comes back: "They were husband and wife." How about Jesus and his disciples? "Well, they were the Savior and his followers."

It is true that we don't generally think of Jesus and his disciples as just a group of friends. Similarly, we don't usually think of Abraham and Sarah, or any of the other married couples in the Bible, in terms of friendship. In fact, we don't typically think of marriage in terms of friendship. A small town newspaper once inadvertently dramatized the point by an article that told of a couple in the town who had recently wed, "thus ending a long friendship."

Yet any intimate relationship, whether romantic or not, is a friendship. Jesus told his disciples at one point that they should love one another and that the greatest love of all is to lay down one's life for one's friends. He went on to say: "You are my friends if you do what I command you. I do not call you servants any longer, because the servant does not know what the master is doing; but I have called you friends" (John 15:14-15). By calling us friends, Jesus stresses the intimacy of our relationship with him.

Marriage, of course, is something more than friendship, but it is always precarious unless it is also a friendship. And in the best marriages, the partners are best friends. Again and again, people in long-term, satisfying marriages have told us that their spouse is their best friend. What that means is "I am in an intimate relationship with someone I like as a person and enjoy being with." Here is the way one wife summed it up:

> I feel that we are the best of friends as well as lovers and parents. I really like my husband. I like the kind of person he is. In fact, even if we were not married, I would want to know him and have him as a friend. He's the kind of person I enjoy being around.

I Like You, Therefore We Are

I think, therefore I am. Whether Descartes was right is debatable. But we are certain of the validity of the marital maxim: I like you, therefore we are. And therefore we shall continue to be. You can't love someone over the long run if you don't like the kind of person he or she is. "Yes, I really love my husband," a wife told us, "but it was the liking that helped us get through the times I wanted to wring his neck." And a man married twenty years said of his wife: "She is the best friend I have. I would rather spend time with her, talk with her, be with her than anyone else."

What exactly do happily married people like about their mates? Is the list endless, or are there some common themes? Actually, a number of qualities are mentioned repeatedly by people.

1. *My spouse gets more interesting over time.* "I know you like the back of my hand." We often hear that kind of statement from someone in a troubled marriage. And it usually means: "You can't fool me. I know what you're doing and why you're doing it." In a good marriage, you know each other well. But since you are both changing, you are never a completely open book to each other, and you do not become bored with each other (a problem mentioned by about a fourth of people who divorce).

Ted has been married thirty-five years. He told us how his wife has become more interesting over time: "She constantly surprises me and impresses me with skills I didn't know she had. I recently watched her chair a committee. It was the first time she ever did it, and she was superb! I didn't think it was possible, but I find her more impressive now than I did when we were married."

2. *My spouse is a good person.* Is love, like justice, blind? Do people in strong marriages see their partners through the distorted eyes of love? Undoubtedly, evaluations are colored by commitment and love. However, most spouses can readily tell you about the deficiencies of their mates. At the same time, thinking of your spouse as a basically good person greatly enhances the compatibility of the union.

What makes someone a basically good person? The qualities most often mentioned by couples are things like consideration, generosity, and integrity. A husband said he likes his wife for many reasons: "First, because she is a kind and compassionate person. She is genuinely concerned about people and their needs. She has an honest, forthright outlook on life."

3. *I enjoy being with, and doing things with, my spouse.* We always cringe when we hear an about-to-be-married couple say such things as: "We give each other plenty of space"; "We don't have to spend all our free time together in order to have fun"; or "We each plan to keep doing things with our own friends." Don't misunderstand us here. We do recognize your need to retain a separate identity, which means at least some activities and some time apart from each other.

At the same time, your spouse is not, or should not be, just one among many friends. Your spouse should be your best friend. This doesn't mean that you prefer to be with your spouse in every single thing you do. For example, Ted, whom we mentioned earlier, said that in at least one situation he and his wife gladly separate:

I hate shopping. She loves it. I used to go with her. She tells me I would hover gloomily behind her the whole time. I really spoiled it for her. We finally agreed, after about twenty years of this, that I would no longer go shopping with her. We're very busy people, and we don't like being apart any more than we have to. But that's one form of togetherness that was agony for both of us.

4. *My spouse and I laugh and have fun together.* Laughter is medicine for your body. It literally facilitates healing and makes you more resistant to health problems. Laughter is also medicine for your marriage. A laugh a day can help keep the therapist away. Laughing together increases intimacy and adds luster and vitality to your relationship.

We know a wife who daily looks for cartoons or other humorous pieces that she can share with her husband so that they can laugh together. Her marriage, she said, is "wonderful." She and her husband have had their share of problems. But humor has been a great help in coping with the troubled times: "Laughter relieves tension and a sense of humor helps one keep a sense of proportion. Laughing together, as well as struggling together, helps to strengthen bonds. But without laughter, the suffering seems pointless."

In addition to laughter, having fun means a certain amount of playfulness in the marriage. Be careful here. For some people, playfulness takes the form of teasing. But there is a thin and often unclear line between teasing as playfulness and teasing as abuse. The following exchange took place between a couple in counseling:

She: You sometimes make remarks that really put me down.
He: What are you talking about? I wouldn't do that.
She: What about the times you tell me that I'm going to be just like my mother when I get older? I can't

help it if she's so grouchy. And I have no intention of becoming like her.

He: Oh, that. I'm only teasing to get you out of a bad mood.

She: But it hurts me when you say it.

The husband defined his words as a form of playfulness that would help his wife. She defined them as hurtful and insensitive, even though she acknowledged that he said them in a playful way. The point is, it's not playfulness unless both partners regard it as such.

What is playfulness? It's many different things to different people. You have to know your partner well in order to be playful with him or her. It can be verbal:

He: I love you.

She: I love you more.

He: But I love you even more than that.

She: That's not possible.

It can also be physical. Couples have fun at everything from spraying each other with a garden hose to wrestling to see who washes and who dries the dishes. Whatever works for you, do it. Just be certain that it works for your spouse as well.

===

Being alike. Friendship. Liking. Now that we have all the ingredients, let's see how we can control the process. What can you and your spouse do to maintain and even increase your compatibility? The following suggestions will help you to become more alike, or intensify the friendship aspect of your relationship, or increase the liking you have for each other.

RX FOR COUPLES: INCREASE YOUR COMPATIBILITY

1. Focus on the positive.
2. Affirm your spouse.
3. Expand your list of shared activities.
4. Make yourself more likable to your spouse.

Read on for more explanation.

---

1. Focus on the positive. Whenever you look at anything or anyone, you select certain things on which to focus. Psychologists call it selective perception. The point is, you can't possibly take in everything, so you select a limited number of points to notice. This means that two people can look at the same thing and focus on different or even contradictory aspects. One person looks at a flower garden and finds it hard to enjoy the flowers because of the weeds. Another looks at the same garden, passes quickly over the weeds, and exults in the beauty of the flowers.

People with long-term, satisfying marriages are like the person who sees the flowers rather than the weeds. They have what we call positive selection. They are not ignorant of the deficiencies of their partners, but they choose to focus on the positive. A husband put it this way: "When I married I figured it was for life. I knew my wife-to-be, and liked what I knew. She is not perfect, but her weak points, which are very few, are of no concern to me. Her strong points overwhelm them."

2. Affirm your spouse. It is one thing to notice and remind yourself about your spouse's positive qualities. It is another and equally important thing to let your spouse know about these qualities and the fact that you appreciate them. A husband put it this way: "I've paid my wife thousands of unspoken compliments. I'm working now on turning them into spoken compliments."

Friends affirm each other. We like people who affirm us. Again, this is not to ignore or gloss over deficiencies. But most spouses are less likely to ignore deficiencies than they are to appreciate positive qualities in silence. To understand the importance of affirmation, think about how you feel when your spouse says one or more of the following kinds of things to you: "I really appreciate the way you helped me today"; "That was really a good dinner"; "I love the way you hold my arm when you talk to me"; "That outfit looks great on you"; "You really impressed me when you defended your views to our friends." There are countless ways in which spouses can affirm each other on a daily basis. Each affirmation adds some glue to the relationship and a touch of joy to the moment.

Public affirmations are also important. We have noticed the look on people's faces—often amounting to something of a glow—when their spouses publicly say praiseworthy things about them. We are not talking about things that sound like boasting, but the same kind of affirmations noted above. "Ken is really helpful with the children," a career-involved wife pointed out to a group of friends. "He's such a good father." Ken's face showed his deep appreciation of her remark.

3. Expand your list of shared activities. Friendships develop because people enjoy doing the same things. We often have particular friends for particular activities—a prayer partner, a fishing buddy, a coffee klatch of friends who enjoy talking together. You are bound together by these shared activities.

One of the reasons you married your spouse was because you enjoyed doing certain things together. We suggest that you continue to expand the activities that you share. One way is to plan, on a regular basis, to do something new together. A regular basis could be anything from weekly to quarterly. What you do may be something that one or both of you have done previously, but you have never done it together. Or it may be something entirely new for both of you.

Paul and Sarah, married less than a year, are committed to a lifelong union. Yet they are having some problems at present because work schedules leave them little time together. The problem is compounded by another fact—Paul is a golfing enthusiast. "Does Sarah also play?" we asked. The answer was no, she had never played. Clearly, Paul was reluctant to take her with him, knowing that as a beginner she would sorely try his patience and undoubtedly dissolve the foursome of which Paul was a part.

We had to be blunt with Paul. Golf, we told him, is an enjoyable activity. But in committing himself to Sarah in marriage, he pledged not to allow anyone or anything to become intrusive. He had, in effect, given his relationship with Sarah priority over every other human activity, human demand, and human relationship. Now he faces a serious test of that commitment. If there is no other way to have time with Sarah, is he willing to alter his golfing pattern?

We'd like to report that Paul now takes Sarah along, or that he goes with Sarah some of the time and his golfing buddies at other times, or that he has cut back on the time he spends golfing. We'd like to report that his decision has brought them closer together. But Paul hasn't made his decision yet. He and Sarah, who calls herself a golf widow, are still struggling.

As you try to expand the list of activities you share, you probably won't like some of the things you try. It's possible that Paul would not enjoy playing golf with Sarah. It's also possible that he would have found it a good deal of fun to teach her and watch her develop. He may never know. For most couples, we believe there will be adventure in trying new, shared activities even though they will not want to repeat some of them.

4. *Make yourself more likable to your spouse.* The emphasis here is on "more" and "to your spouse." That means that there is room for improvement in all of us, and it means that you focus on the things that appeal to your spouse.

We suggest two ways to make yourself more likable. The first is the exercise we suggested at the end of chapter 1— discuss what you really appreciate in each other. Then continue to cultivate those qualities. The other is for each spouse to make a list of what he or she likes generally about people of the opposite sex. What qualities do you admire? What kinds of behavior, including things that are said, impress you?

When you see what your spouse admires in other people, you see the kinds of qualities you may want to develop or nurture in yourself. For instance, maybe your spouse admires those who have a good sense of humor. This is a quality you can cultivate and, in the process, make yourself more likable to your spouse.

However, it's not always an easy task. The demands and challenges and frustrations of everyday life can sometimes crowd humor out. A husband told us of an interesting conversation he had with a colleague at work. After working well together for a number of years, they talked one day about their initial impressions of each other: "When I asked him what he thought of me when we first started working together, his reply was unsettling. He said he thought I was an extremely serious person. That I didn't seem to have much fun. I never thought of myself that way. But I realized that I had let the demands of my life make me more sober than I wanted to be. I went to work on it, both at work and at home."

Other qualities can similarly be cultivated or brought back to life. The point is to bring into your life, or intensify, those qualities that make you ever more likable to your spouse. The payoff is great, because the probability is that they'll make you more likable generally. In any case, they will certainly intensify your attractiveness to your spouse. And that means a sense of increasing compatibility in your marriage for each of you.

EXERCISING COMPATIBILITY

Do the following as a couple or in a group with other couples:

1. Make a list of things you like or admire about your spouse. For the next few weeks, compliment your spouse each time you observe something on the list (it could become habitual).
2. Each month do a fun thing together that you've never done before as a couple.
3. Select one of the following areas and discuss how you and your spouse are alike and how you could become more alike: faith, leisure activities, money, parenting, work, communication.
4. Repeat with each of the other areas. Develop a specific plan for growing more compatible.

5

Communication

A word fitly spoken is like apples of gold in a setting of silver.
—Proverbs 25:11

COMMUNICATION CHECKUP

Answer each of the following questions, then read on to see how your communication affects the health of your marriage.

1. How often do you feel your spouse doesn't understand you, or that the two of you are talking at cross-purposes?
2. To what extent does your communication with your spouse make you feel closer together?
3. How often do you and your spouse speak about your feelings?
4. What would you like your spouse to talk more about with you?
5. How much should your spouse know about your needs or desires without you having to articulate them?

An old story illustrates both the difficulty and the importance of communication. A married couple was relaxing at home one evening. He was watching television.

She was working a crossword puzzle as she watched the program with him. Suddenly she turned to him and said: "Honey, what's a female sheep?" "Ewe," he snapped. And the fight began.

It almost sounds trite to say that communication is a vital part of a healthy marriage, or that effective communication is a challenge. But both things are true. The majority of couples who divorce or who see marriage counselors reports communication problems as at least one of the factors that led to their troubles. The better you communicate before you marry, the more likely you are to have a satisfying marriage. The better you communicate now, the less likely you are in the future to get mired in problems that never seem to get resolved.

We Don't Assume, We Talk

Assumptions are the deadly enemy of marriage. Consider the following situation. Husband and wife come home from work. Both are tired. Both have had frustrating days. He looks preoccupied and sullen. She wants an encouraging word from her husband, but can tell by the look on his face that he is not in a cheery or cheering mood. After the frustrating day at work, she is in no mood for additional difficulties at home. What's the matter with him? Is he mad at her because they didn't make love last night? She decides he is, and that increases her frustration and adds an edge of anger to it. She speaks curtly to him, frowning as she talks: "What do you want to do for dinner?"

Meanwhile, he has also noticed the look on her face, and can't decide if it's weariness or irritation with him. He, too, is in no mood for any confrontation after a trying day at work. He decides that she thinks he is not sensitive enough to her needs and is sending him the message that there will be no lovemaking tonight either. He's too weary anyway, he thinks to himself, but it irritates him that she feels that way. He responds to her question with equal sharpness: "I don't care. I don't even care if we eat."

The situation is both fiction and reality. We made it up. But something like that happens to countless numbers of couples. One or both make assumptions about why the other looks a certain way or talks a certain way. The assumptions create negative moods, which then can generate into angry silences or escalate into a raucous argument.

Communication, therefore, means that we don't make assumptions; instead, we talk. The reason is simple—if we don't talk we will certainly make assumptions. People in an intimate relationship want to know what's going on with their partner. They need to be able to understand their partner's moods. If your partner doesn't tell you why he or she is feeling a certain way, you will make an assumption. Your assumption might be wrong. And it might detract from the quality of your relationship.

The way to avoid getting trapped by assumptions is for you and your spouse each to agree to a fundamental principle: I will not make assumptions about your behavior, and I will not force you to make assumptions about mine by failing to tell you what I am feeling and why I am feeling that way. Like all principles, this one should not be followed rigidly and mindlessly. There may be occasions when assumptions are reasonable and appropriate. For example, we know a woman whose husband always looks grim on Tuesday mornings. Not willing to make assumptions, she questioned him the first few times she noticed it. Subsequent questionings were not necessary, however. His job requires him to be in a Tuesday morning meeting that he finds distasteful. If she asked him every week why he looked grim, the question would only add to his frustration.

Communication Is the Soul of Intimacy

If communication helps you avoid something—assumptions that corrode your relationship—it also helps you to build something—the intimacy that nourishes your life. In fact, communication is the soul of intimacy. To be intimate with someone means to feel bonded to that person. Bonding requires that each person know the other; and you only know someone when he or she shares feelings, hopes, fears, desires, likes, and dislikes with you.

Note that when Jesus called the disciples his friends, he said it was "because I have made known to you everything that I have heard from my Father" (John 15:15). Sharing what you are and what you know is the only way to build intimacy, whether the intimacy of friendship or of marriage.

Obviously, both husband and wife need to share themselves. When that mutual sharing happens, you may notice something interesting. As expressed by a husband: "I knew that when I talked to my wife it made her feel closer to me. One day I told her about some things that happened to me when I was a child. One of them was pretty painful. I had never told anyone else about it. She was very supportive and sympathetic. Reflecting on it afterwards, I was struck by the fact that after sharing my experiences I felt closer to her."

In other words, it's not just that his sharing helps her, and her sharing helps him. Rather, whenever you share something of yourself with your spouse, you get a double dividend—both of you gain in your feeling of intimacy.

What kind of communication builds intimacy? Keep in mind that you need not always share something profound from the depths of your psyche in order to feel closer to your spouse. We often regard small talk as something that people do to pass the time when they are not interested in deepening their relationship. However, small talk is important to marital intimacy. Small talk is a way of maintaining connectedness, of sustaining openness to each other, and of sharing the commonplace as well as the profound.

Communicating Is a Skill

So far it sounds simple—just talk to each other and you will achieve the intimacy you need. That's too simple. Talking doesn't necessarily mean that you are communicating, at least not the kind of communicating that builds intimacy. Effective communication is a skill. There are some things to know and some things to practice in order to communicate well.

1. *Men and women tend to communicate differently.* One of the common complaints of wives is "he doesn't talk to me." In some cases, that means he is too reticent about expressing his feelings. In other cases it just means he doesn't communicate with her the way her female friends do. In either case, husbands and wives need to understand that both individual and gender differences make effective communication challenging. Let's look at the gender differences here.

Psychiatrist Aaron Beck has described one of the fundamental gender differences: a woman tends to think, if we can keep talking about it we can work it out; a man tends to think, if we have to keep talking about it something must be wrong. In other words, women are more likely than men to want to discuss something thoroughly. A wife may find it comforting to talk repeatedly about her marriage as a way to ensure that all is well and to maintain high quality. Her husband, on the other hand, may find repeated discussions of the marriage to be at best pointless and at worst a signal that the relationship is off track.

Communications expert Deborah Tannen has pointed out that other gender differences are rooted in fundamentally different approaches to life. Men tend to treat life as a kind of contest, with the goal being to preserve one's independence and avoid failure. Women tend to think of life as a community affair, with the goal being to maintain intimacy and avoid isolation. Such a difference has consequences for all kinds of situations. For instance, talking with her husband before making a decision may make a woman feel good because it means her life is bound up with someone else's. For a man, however, consulting with his wife before making a decision may make him feel that he has lost his independence. Consequently, husbands are more likely than wives to make decisions without conferring with their partner.

Another important gender difference is the tendency of men to respond to someone's troubles with advice or an effort to solve the problem. Women, in contrast, are more likely to respond with sympathy and understanding.

Fred and Linda illustrate the way in which such differences can cause problems in a marriage. The following is a conversation they had with a counselor:

> Linda: It really irritates me when I tell Fred something that is bothering me and he just tells me what I should do.
> Fred: I'm only trying to help.
> Linda: But that's not what I want. I mean, that's not why I'm telling it to you.
> Counselor: What you really need is someone to hear you out, to let you vent your frustrations or anger or whatever.

Linda: Yes, that's it. That's what I want.

Fred: I think that when something's wrong, you just need to figure out how to make it right.

Counselor: That can often be very helpful, Fred. But listen carefully to what Linda's saying. She doesn't want you to solve her problems. She wants you to give her the opportunity to talk them out. In fact, she needs that from you. If she then wants your advice as well, she'll ask for it.

Fred's typically male approach—to avoid failure and to offer advice—made it difficult for him to even understand Linda's needs. Eventually, he got the point. He's working on a different approach with Linda. In fact, they're working on it together. "He'll slip back into his old mode," Linda told us, "and then I have to remind him that I don't want advice. I just want to talk about it."

One hopes that what Fred will learn is that by talking it out, Linda is solving her own problem. Furthermore, they are building intimacy. Finally, they illustrate an important point—to say that men and women tend to have, or typically have, differing communication styles is not to say that the differences are either immutable or inevitably damaging. We can all learn to change our styles and talk together in a way that enhances intimacy.

2. *Compassionate listening is essential to communication.* After an hour's premarital session with a couple, each of whom acknowledged a love for talking, the counselor said: "I want you to think seriously about what's happened in here today. I'm the only person in the room who has been listening. You talk to each other, but you don't listen. I've heard two monologues, but very little dialogue."

Listening is essential for effective communication. It is essential for intimacy, because we all need to be listened to.

Listening is work, because it requires you to give the other person full opportunity to express himself or herself and to strive to understand what the person is saying. We tend to put most of our energy into trying to get others to understand us; it is equally important to put energy into trying to understand others.

You may have heard the phrase "active listening." It stresses the need to put effort into the listening process. We prefer the term "compassionate listening," which stresses the need to both understand and care about what the other is saying. You can care without understanding, and understand without caring. You only build intimacy in marriage when you both understand and care.

Compassionate listening means that you are sensitive to the nonverbal as well as the verbal. Your spouse may be troubled by something that you regard as trivial. If you see a look of pain on your spouse's face after something you said, you have a strong and clear message to examine the content of what you said and how you said it.

Compassionate listening requires you to focus on your spouse and what your spouse is saying. You need to resist distractions. You must resist the temptation to allow something your spouse says to trigger another train of thought. Even if you start thinking about an appropriate response, you are no longer listening.

In the case of Fred and Linda, Fred's advice was not only unwanted but sometimes inappropriate because he didn't hear her out. For example, she told of a time when she started telling him about a problem with her supervisor at work. He interrupted her with: "Take it to the next level; you don't have to tolerate that kind of treatment." She asked him to please let her finish, then explained how she had worked the situation out with her supervisor without taking it to the next level and causing more serious problems. Linda didn't need his advice; she only needed him to listen to what had happened and to affirm her course of action. What Fred never realized was that his habit of giving quick advice sent an unintended message to Linda: "I don't care that much about what you're saying to me; here's a way to deal with it so we don't have to talk about it anymore." He was not a compassionate listener, because he didn't seem to care enough to hear Linda out. He really does care, of course, and is learning how to communicate that to Linda by honing his listening skills.

3. *Articulate what's going on within you.* Most of the couples with whom we talk acknowledge that one of the partners has some difficulty in expressing feelings. Usually it's the husband, but sometimes it's the wife. The problem may be compounded by the fact that the individual grew up in a family that did not encourage the expression of feelings. Alice is an example of a wife who has a problem expressing feelings—in her case, negative feelings. Her husband, Bob, finds it easy to show and talk about feelings. Bob's parents encouraged everyone in the family to be honest about how they felt and to react emotionally to events. By contrast, Alice's parents taught her both in words and in deeds that one's feelings are to be kept to oneself. When she got angry as a child, they would put her in her room until she no longer acted angry. They never talked about why she was angry; they simply isolated her until she could act and talk without anger. The pattern continued. In fact, when she fell in love with Bob, her parents cautioned her: "Don't show your feelings, or you might ruin the relationship." They didn't even want her to reveal how excited she was to be in love with Bob! It is little wonder that Alice struggles now with expressing feelings.

You don't need to share all your feelings with your spouse. A passing irritation or annoyance with one's spouse, a brief feeling of lust for someone else, or a momentary yearning for singlehood are examples of feelings that are usually best left unspoken. But communication can't be complete without some awareness of how a spouse feels as well as how he or she thinks about a matter.

That is a point that Bob is teaching Alice. When they attended a funeral of a close relative, Alice got tears in her eyes. Her mother told her not to cry. Bob, sitting on the other side, whispered to her, "It's okay to cry." When he senses that Alice is upset or depressed or angry, he insists that she talk to him about it. For instance:

We were coming out of a store one day, and I was feeling upset with him for something he had said. He could sense it. He asked what was wrong, but I would only say "Nothing." When we got to the car, he literally picked me up and sat me on the trunk and said we were not moving until I told him what was wrong. I really appreciate that about him. I'm learning how to tell him how I feel. And I'm finding out how liberating it is and how important it is to marriage.

To some extent, we reveal our feelings nonverbally through facial expressions and body posture. But since a particular nonverbal signal could express more than one emotion, the failure to verbalize feelings means that the spouse is forced to make assumptions. The bottom line is, any effective communication requires you to tell your partner both what you think about something and how you feel about it.

Because effective communication is a learned skill, there are a number of ways that you can improve. "Improve," incidentally, doesn't mean you are inadequate now. The point is that no matter how well you communicate now, you can always enhance your skill in this crucial area of marriage.

RX FOR COUPLES: IMPROVE YOUR COMMUNICATION

1. Practice self-disclosure.
2. Reward your spouse's communication efforts.
3. Keep a communication log for several weeks.
4. Hone your listening skills.

Read on for more explanation.

1. Practice self-disclosure. As we noted, at least one partner in a marriage frequently has trouble with self-disclosure, especially with feelings. Keeping in mind that self-disclosure does not mean sharing everything all the time, the partner who has difficulty in this area will be helped by a simple exercise of mutual sharing. The partner who finds it easier should begin, talking to the other about himself or herself for five to ten minutes. During that time, the listening partner says nothing. And the talking partner cannot talk about anyone else or even about the marital relationship—only about himself or herself. At the end of the time, the roles are reversed. After each partner has finished, they discuss together what has been said and what they have learned about the other.

For people who have a problem sharing feelings, here is another simple exercise. Select a topic of interest to each of you, one that generates some emotion like money, in-laws, enjoyable leisure activities, a momentous event in your lives, and so forth. Then each of you in turn tells the other in detail the feelings you experience about that topic or activity or event. Include a description of how those feelings affected you mentally and physically. This exercise will sensitize you to become more aware of your feelings and also help you to articulate them more fully.

2. *Reward your spouse's communication efforts.* How often has something like the following happened to you?

She: You look a bit upset today. Anything wrong?
He: I'm okay.
She: But something seems to be bothering you.
He: I guess I feel guilty about not calling my mother yesterday. But we were so busy.
She: (*Curtly*) You shouldn't feel guilty.
He: (*Silence*)

If he has difficulty acknowledging his negative feelings, she has just made it even more difficult by telling him that his feelings are wrong. She has, in effect, punished him for being honest with her and made it less likely that he will be open about his feelings in the future.

Alice had this experience with a boyfriend she had before she met Bob. "He always assumed that we would marry," she told us, "but the longer we were together the less I wanted to be married to him." When she tried a number of times to explain to him that she no longer had strong feelings for him—something that was extremely difficult for her to do—he got angry and told her: "You're wrong. You don't know how you feel." The relationship only worsened Alice's problem with expressing her feelings.

Bob, in contrast, rewards Alice's efforts. Recall that he told her it was okay for her to cry at the funeral. And when she is able to share negative feelings with him, he reminds her that they are now "walking the same way down the street again" because they both know what is going on.

To return to the example, "you shouldn't feel that way" is a common but counterproductive response. How else could she have responded to her husband? Here's a possible scenario:

She: Tell me why you feel guilty.
He: I know my mother expects me to call every Saturday. I know she's disappointed that I didn't.
She: And that bothers you.
He: Very much. I guess it's silly. I usually call every week, but we were just so busy all day.
She: We really were. Don't you think she'll understand that?

And so on. In this scenario, the wife is showing understanding and caring. She encourages her husband to continue talking. She could cap off the discussion by saying something like: "I really appreciate you telling me what was bothering you. I feel more like we're a team."

3. *Keep a communication log for several weeks.* Instead of just estimating what kind of communication you have, try keeping a daily record for a number of weeks. For each day, write down how long you speak with each other and the topics you discuss. Then assess the results.

You may discover some surprises. We asked a marriage enrichment group to do this for a week. When we met again, one couple said: "We realize that we are so busy during the week that we are trying to cram a week's worth of talk into the weekend." Another reported: "We found out that the bulk of our talking centers around the children."

To assess your own log, answer the following questions:

• Do you have a good balance of small talk and more significant topics?

• Do you cover a range of topics or tend to give the bulk of your time to a single topic like the children or work?

• Is there enough self-disclosure to maintain and build intimacy?

• Is there enough discussion of your relationship to make you feel that you are nurturing your marriage?

• To what extent does your communication support and affirm each other?

When your assessment is complete, you can work together on a plan to make improvements. For example, if you decide that you are spending too much time on one topic, think about how you can expand the range of subjects you discuss. Perhaps you can talk more about items in the daily news, or more about your hopes and aspirations for the future. You can tell each other about a book you are reading, or you can both read the same book and discuss it. At whatever point you sense a need or a possibility for improvement, you can probably come up with a number of potential ways to achieve more satisfying communication with your spouse.

4. *Hone your listening skills.* Because Alice has trouble articulating her own feelings, she doesn't always under-stand Bob's. He uses an excellent method for improving the listening process. Instead of repeatedly explaining to Alice what he is feeling, he stops and asks her to tell him how he feels. If she doesn't get it right, he explains again and then has her try once again.

You can improve your own listening by saying to your partner: "Let me see if I understand you. You are saying . . ." You can improve your partner's listening by saying: "Just to make sure we are on track here, you tell me what I am trying to say."

Another way to improve listening and to let your spouse know that he or she is heard is always to respond verbally to any communication. A grunt, a shake of the head, or a murmured "Hmm" will not be acceptable. Even if your partner engages in small talk, like "It is a beautiful day," you should respond verbally: "I agree. I love this kind of weather."

Verbal responses, incidentally, help turn mere listening into compassionate listening. You care enough about what your partner says, even about relatively trivial statements, to put energy into a response. That means a lot. Two people who are compassionate listeners are continually affirming and nurturing each other. They are practicing healthy communication, and their marriage will benefit accordingly.

EXERCISING COMMUNICATION

Do the following as a couple or in a group with other couples:

1. Practice self-disclosure by talking about one of your most painful and one of your most enjoyable experiences as a child. Try to recapture the full range of feelings you had at the time.
2. Tell about one of the most enjoyable conversations you ever had. What made it so gratifying?
3. Practice listening by having your partner tell you in detail an emotional experience. Retell the experience in detail, and ask your partner to check your accuracy.
4. Name the kinds of things that are hardest and easiest for you to talk about. Discuss why they are hard or easy and explore ways to make the difficult ones more palatable.

6

*C*oupling

I am my beloved's, and his desire is for me.
—Song of Solomon 7:10

COUPLING CHECKUP

Answer each of the following questions, then read on to see how coupling affects the health of your marriage.

1. How many adjectives can you list that describe what the word *sex* means to you?
2. What do you expect to happen in your sexual relationship over the next ten years?
3. How would you describe the ideal sex life?
4. In what ways do you and your spouse differ in terms of sexual needs?
5. How important are sexual relations to a healthy marriage?

hy not just say "sex"? Why use the term *coupling*? First, *coupling* is a term used by some sex experts. Second, we think it describes well what happens in satisfying sex in a good marriage. Coupling figuratively describes an act in which two people are emotionally as well as physically joined in union without destroying their individual identities. Finally, in our culture the word *sex* puts the emphasis on the individual's needs; the word *coupling* puts the emphasis on the relationship.

Having said all that, we will—for the sake of variety—use both terms, *sex* and *coupling*. But in a sex-focused culture in which the emphasis is frequently on sex for sex's sake, we think the term *coupling* has much to be said for it.

What Is the Purpose of Coupling?

Why do people engage in sexual relations? Why did God create human sexuality? In other words, where does it lead us if we look at sexuality from a purely human point of view and then from God's point of view? We believe that it leads to the same conclusion, and that conclusion is necessary if coupling is to be an enriching part of your marriage. Let's explore the issue.

1. *The sex drive is strong, but not beyond control.* We all agree that the sex drive is basic and strong. Some people go beyond that and argue that sexual relations are imperative for their well-being. A young husband, struggling with his wife's diminished desire after their child was born, put it this way: "For her, sex is just one *more* thing you have to do at the end of the day. For me, sex is just one more thing you *have* to do at the end of the day."

The husband believed that the quality of his marriage was suffering because of a lack of sexual relations. He needed to couple with his wife. We don't doubt his sense of need, but we pose a question. Was his need created solely by his own genetic makeup, or does it also reflect his culture? There are, for example, some cultures in which spouses have no sexual relations for one to two years after a child is born. Are they biologically different from us? Do they have different sexual needs? The answer, of course, is no, they simply have different cultural rules and expectations.

We live in a culture that compounds the issue of sexuality by portraying sexual relations as a fundamental human right and an integral part of human happiness. In our culture, "healthy celibate" is an oxymoron and "fornication" is a term for archaic morality. To be married and sexually frustrated at times because your partner "doesn't feel like it" is a form of gross injustice and intolerable deprivation.

The point is, if coupling is to enhance rather than vex your marriage, you need to be realistic about your sexual drive. Paul had a realistic view in his advice to the Corinthians: "The husband should give to his wife her conjugal rights, and likewise the wife to her husband. . . . Do not deprive one another except perhaps by agreement for a set time, to devote yourselves to prayer, and then come together again" (1 Cor. 7:3, 5).

In essence, Paul reminds us that the sex drive is strong, that each partner should be considerate of the sexual needs of the other, and that there may be reasons for mutually agreeing to a time of abstinence, but it should not be an extended or open-ended period of time. The message of our culture is: *you* should be sexually fulfilled. The biblical message is: you and your spouse should work together for mutual fulfillment. The cultural message assumes that your sexual needs are imperative and tells you to focus on your own needs. The biblical message assumes that your sexual needs are strong but controllable, and tells you to focus on your spouse's needs as well as your own.

2. Coupling has many functions. For many centuries, theologians asserted that the primary purpose of sex is procreation. God made us sexual creatures in order that we might populate the earth. Eventually, a contrasting argument emerged—sex is for pleasure and fulfillment, not simply for procreation.

Both arguments have merit. Sexual intercourse is the usual way to procreate, and God's command to humans from the very beginning was: "Be fruitful and multiply, and fill the earth and subdue it" (Gen. 1:28). But sex is obviously a source of pleasure, and Paul's advice to the Corinthians was not based upon the need to procreate. Rather, he urged them not to neglect each other's sexual needs "so that Satan may not tempt you because of your lack of self-control" (1 Cor. 7:5). Paul knew that humans need sexual relations for more reasons than to have children.

Beyond procreation and pleasure, we engage in sex for a variety of other reasons. Charlotte and Stan have been married for twelve years. They have confronted the sexual challenges that most couples face and have considerable insight into the meaning of coupling for their relationship. Stan, for instance, knows that sexual relations help relieve the tensions of living:

> When we don't have sex for awhile, I get more irritable. I have less patience. And it happens to Charlotte, too. She gets more sharp, more short-tempered with me. But after we have sex, we're both more easygoing, more patient.

Charlotte agrees with Stan. In addition, she told us, coupling is important to her feelings about herself:

> Sex makes me feel good about myself as well as about our marriage. If we don't have sex for awhile, I begin to wonder about how lovable, how attractive, I am.

When we have sex, I know I am wanted, I am loved, I am needed.

Clearly, coupling is a powerful tool for fulfilling many different needs. We should note that it can also be misused. You misuse sex if you employ it for personal advantage, withholding or granting sexual relations as a way to control your partner's behavior. Paul's point to the Corinthians was that any period of abstinence should be by mutual consent. But what if you are angry with your spouse, or if you have no desire at a time your spouse wants to have sexual relations? Then it's time for some healthy communication. Charlotte made an interesting observation about how she and Stan communicate when one of them is sexually aroused and the other isn't:

> We are well adjusted to each other sexually. But we don't always want sex at the same time. When that happens, we're pretty open with each other. For instance, I might say to Stan: "I don't feel in the mood tonight; I'm really tired. But I'm willing if you really want to. Or if you want to wait, I'll probably be more in the mood in the morning." Depending on how strong his need is, Stan will either wait or we'll go ahead and have sex.

Note that Charlotte told Stan three important things. First, she told him about her own sexual feelings at the time. Second, she told him, in effect, that she was concerned about his sexual needs. And third, she told him she would work with him to find a mutually agreeable answer. With that kind of communication, your chances of sexual fulfillment are greatly enhanced.

3. *The primary purpose of coupling is union.* Although we
have noted many functions of coupling, we have not yet
identified what we believe is its primary function, namely,
union. The Genesis account of creation talks about man's
sense of incompleteness without woman, and of God's call
for a man and woman to become "one flesh" (Gen. 2:24).
The fundamental purpose of marriage is union between two
people. And sexual intercourse is one of the tools for
achieving the intimate union that is at the heart of our
wholeness.

We all need intimacy. We begin our existence in the
nurturing intimacy of our mother's womb. As growing
infants, we gain a sense of security and well-being in
intimacy with parents. Intimate friends affirm us and help
us develop a sense of competence to deal with our world.
The intimacy of marriage sustains and enriches us as we
mature. Intimacy with God circumscribes our existence
with meaning and nourishes us with guidance, strength,
and hope.

Each kind of intimacy is to some extent unique and
special. Marital intimacy, the "one flesh" of Genesis, involves self-disclosure, sharing, trust, and commitment to
an extent that is unique in human relationships. Such
intimacy makes us vulnerable, which explains why break-
ups tend to be so fierce and agonizing. But it also contributes a great deal to our emotional and physical health, to
our ability to cope with challenges and stress, and to our
capacity to find meaning and zest in life.

Coupling is one of the tools for achieving the intimate
union of marriage. Actually, some people try to gain the
intimate union, or at least the benefits of that union, apart
from marriage. They search for meaning and fulfillment
through sexual encounters, but the search is in vain. Psy-

chotherapists point out that one-night stands and other kinds of impersonal sex not only fail to fulfill people's intimacy needs but also leave them feeling more isolated and lonely than they were before the sex.

The way in which marital coupling is a part of creating intimate union is described by a man married for twenty years:

> When we were first married, I thought about sex as just great pleasure, one of the major benefits of marriage. As the years pass, though, I realize that sex is far more than that. It connects us in a special way, a way that neither of us is connected to anyone else in the world. I once heard someone talk about sex as a mystery. I never understood that until I had been married for a few years. Now I do. In some mysterious way, sex binds you to each other in your own private world.

That special connectedness is the primary purpose of sex. Coupling—at its best—is an act of love between two people who have achieved a mysterious oneness of being ("mysterious" because, though they are one, they have not lost their individual identities) and who are both expressing and strengthening their oneness.

How Important Is Coupling to Marriage?

A man answered the question by observing that he never met anyone who expected to be both married and celibate. And what we have said so far would seem to make sexual relations essential to any good marriage. But we need to qualify what we have said with two observations. First, we stated that coupling is one of the tools for achieving intimate union. And second, there can be good sex in a bad marriage and bad sex or even no sex in a good marriage. What exactly, then, is the role of coupling in marriage?

1. *Coupling is important, but not the most crucial element in marriage.* Two examples illustrate the point. The first is a young man who was studying to be a counselor when we met him. He announced proudly one day that he was getting married. We congratulated him and asked him to tell us about his future wife. The more he talked, the more uneasy we felt. What it finally boiled down to was that the two of them had "great sex" together, but had little else in common. In fact, much of the time that they were not having their great sex, they were bickering. Our efforts to help him see what he was doing were to no avail. He married her. In less than a year, they were divorced. "Great sex" could not hold the marriage together.

The second illustration involves a woman married twenty-five years. It is her second marriage and she is "extremely happy" in it. For the last ten years, however, there has been no sex in her marriage. It is not what she would prefer. And it hasn't always been that way. The sexual relations stopped after her husband had a serious operation:

> Important to my adjustment to this is that I was once married before where the marriage was almost totally sex and little else. So I suppose a kind of trade-off exists here—I like absolutely everything else about my current marriage.

In other words, satisfying sexual relations won't hold a bad marriage together, nor will the lack of satisfying sexual relations doom a good marriage. Yet in the most satisfying marriages, coupling is an important part of achieving the fulfilling union that the Bible calls "one flesh."

2. Different patterns of coupling are found in satisfying marriages. "I assumed when I got married," a woman told us, "that I would have sex whenever I wanted to. It only took a few weeks to dispel that illusion." Like most of us, the woman discovered that she had married someone whose sexual drive was not a perfect match for her own. A good deal of frustration and conflict would be eliminated if everyone married someone with the exact same sexual drive. Hardly anyone does.

As a result, part of the challenge of building a satisfying marriage is to find a mutually satisfying pattern of coupling. You and your spouse probably differ in your preferences on such matters as how often, where, and what kind of techniques to use.

Keep in mind the basic purpose of coupling (to help achieve intimate union) as you strive to find a mutually satisfying pattern. Remember there is no single pattern that is the most satisfying for all couples. In our research with couples married fifteen years or more, we found three different patterns of frequency (after the first phase of marriage when sexual activity is likely to be at its peak) among those with happy marriages: a tendency to decline, a tendency to remain stable, and a tendency for some increase. The point is, there is no single right way or best way to engage in coupling. The challenge is not to make your own pattern close to some ideal set up by someone else. The challenge is to make your pattern work for you, so that your coupling helps you achieve intimate union.

We heard an expert on human sexuality declare that, after more than three decades as a sex therapist, he could state confidently that the best sex is married sex. Married people who are faithful to their spouses, he observed, sometimes think that either singles or unfaithful married people are having exotic experiences that the faithful are missing. It isn't true. The most satisfying coupling occurs between married people who are faithful to each other.

═══

What happens to the quality of sexual relations as you age? That all depends. The quality of our sexual lives does not necessarily or inevitably decline. A woman married forty years told us that her sex life was "better than ever." You can make that happen in your marriage, and you can begin the process of improvement immediately.

RX FOR COUPLES: ENHANCE THE QUALITY OF YOUR COUPLING

1. Make coupling part of an intimate process, not simply an act.
2. Work through gender and individual differences in your sexuality.
3. Explore the varied facets of coupling, including what works and what doesn't for you and your spouse.
4. Patiently and creatively work together to maintain regular sexual encounters.

Read on for more explanation.

1. Make coupling part of an intimate process, not simply an act. In a real and fundamental sense, you have to build a better relationship in order to build a better sex life. Everything you do that improves the quality of your relationship, from talking to shared leisure pursuits, will add to the quality of your coupling. A therapist told us that he urges the couples he sees to get involved in some kind of meaningful, shared activity. Attending church together or volunteering your services to service organizations are activities that create a greater sense of connectedness and oneness that spills over into a richer sex life.

Ongoing expressions of affection are a particularly important part of the intimate process. Charlotte says that her sex life is so satisfying because it is an extension of what generally goes on in her relationship with Stan:

> Even though we've been married for twelve years now, Stan is still as attentive as ever. We kiss and hug every day. We touch each other a lot. That's really important to me. Little things like holding hands, or having him caress my arm make me feel warm. They kind of build up to a point where you just have to express your feelings in sex.

Be cautious, however. Your aim should really be to enhance the quality of your relationship generally, and not merely to do the things necessary to get better or more sex. A husband admitted that his efforts to be more affectionate backfired because it was clear to his wife that he only wanted sexual relations more frequently. "And was that true?" we asked. "Yes," he admitted:

> My mind is still on my business a lot of the time I'm home. I just don't think about things like showing affection. But I decided to be more attentive on evenings when I wanted to have sex. She saw through that one right away, and it only made things worse.

The man's focus was still on the act rather than on the process. It's only when you truly work on the intimate process that the quality of coupling grows.

2. Work through gender and individual differences in your sexuality. Both gender and individual differences exist in sexuality. A common belief is that "he" desires more frequent sex than "she" does. But there are individual differences. We know many couples in which the wife prefers sex more frequently than does the husband. In any case, you are most likely in a marriage in which one of you desires more frequent coupling than does the other. It is helpful to keep in mind that few, if any, couples are perfectly matched on the issue of frequency. It is one of those challenges that you need to confront and work through. Working through it includes identifying the problem (are the differences innate or due to differing schedules or rooted in too little ongoing affection, and so on?); listing as many alternative ways to deal with the problem as possible; and deciding which alternative to try first (if it doesn't work, you will want to try another).

Another common challenge is the tendency of women to feel sexy as a result of ongoing affection and the tendency of men to feel affectionate as a result of ongoing sex. A husband identified this as one of the problems he and his wife, Phyllis, had to face and overcome:

> I admit that I don't feel as close to Phyllis when we don't have sex for awhile. I withdraw. That only makes it less likely that we will make love. I have to fight that, and remind myself that Phyllis needs the sex too, that she isn't the one to blame, and that it's not solely her responsibility to make sure we have sex regularly. She helps a lot because she knows how I get, and she's gracious enough to overlook my less than appealing behavior when I'm sexually frustrated.

The man makes an important point: as in all marital matters, dealing with sexual differences and problems is a mutual responsibility. And that means open discussion in which you work together to solve the problem (see the next chapter, on methods of handling conflict).

3. Explore the varied facets of coupling, including what works and what doesn't for you and your spouse. We heard a wise counselor say that one of the challenges married couples face is how to keep sex from becoming boring. He's right. On the one hand, we have already pointed out that some couples report fulfilling coupling after decades of faithful marriage. On the other hand, some couples lose sexual interest in each other. A young wife told us that no one can have satisfying sex with the same person for more than about five years (she is now divorced).

So how do you maintain an interesting and even exciting sex life? We suggest two things. First, read one or more of the good books available on sexual techniques. In fact, try reading them together. Talk about your reactions to what you read. Get a sense of what appeals to you and your spouse. Decide on what you would like to try in your own lovemaking. The point is to add some variety, to make your coupling something that has some element of surprise or newness to it rather than something that follows a pre-scribed and known script.

Second, we suggest that you each make notes about the kinds of things that you find particularly arousing and satisfying and those that you don't. Share your notes with each other. This suggestion is based on the assumption that you may find it difficult to talk directly about what you prefer to do or not to do during coupling (in spite of the sexual openness of our society, we find many people who are embarrassed to talk openly and frankly about sex with their spouses). If you and your spouse can discuss sexual matters freely and honestly with each other, then talk instead of making notes. For example: "It really turns me on when you . . ."

4. *Patiently and creatively work together to maintain regular sexual encounters.* One of the more difficult times sexually for couples is during the child-rearing years, when the time and energy demands of parenting make exciting coupling encounters difficult at best. Demanding work schedules may also make it difficult to maintain the kind of sex life you would like whether or not you have children. A common complaint among dual-career couples is the lack of time and energy for sex, a lack that may involve one or both partners.

With patience and creativity, you can work together to maintain some regularity in your coupling. Here are a few examples of what couples have told us:

> We were getting ready for work one morning, both of us in the bathroom half-naked. I looked at my wife and felt excited. I started caressing her. She looked at me, and we just jumped back into bed and had a "quickie." We've had a lot of quickies since then. They're no substitute for regular lovemaking. But, believe me, they're a lot better than waiting until we have more time, and they keep us on track sexually.

> I grew up with the idea that sex is something you do after dark and under covers. When my husband and I started thinking about seizing any opportunity, we began making love more often. We've even gotten up early in the morning and made love before breakfast.

We plan it. We look over our schedule each week and mark out the times when we can make love. Sometimes it's hard to get turned on when it's not spontaneous. But sometimes the anticipation makes it all the more enjoyable.

Work, children, moods, and various responsibilities combine to make it unlikely that you will ever have sexual relations whenever you prefer. But with patience and creative working together, you and your spouse can make coupling a rich and enriching part of your marital journey.

EXERCISING HEALTHY COUPLING

Do the following as a couple or in a group with other couples:

1. Plan a weekend away together. Make it a time when you are completely absorbed in each other.
2. Make a list of twenty ways to express affection to your partner. Start practicing them.
3. Write an erotic letter to your spouse.

7

*C*onflict

Be angry but do not sin; do not let the sun go down on your anger.
—*Ephesians 4:26*

CONFLICT CHECKUP

Answer each of the following questions, then read on to see how conflict affects the health of your marriage.

1. If you have a good Christian marriage, you won't have conflict. True or false?
2. What are the sources of conflict in your marriage?
3. How many benefits of conflict can you identify?
4. Do you and your spouse argue productively? Why or why not?
5. When you argue, do old issues keep coming up?

*Y*ou may be surprised that we list conflict as an essential of a healthy marriage. Isn't it the lack of conflict that your marriage really needs? To be sure, conflict can tear a relationship apart. But so can the lack of conflict. The total absence of conflict may mean that the partners don't even care enough about each other or their relationship to bother with arguments! People who do care, on the other hand, are going to have disagreements. As a woman with a strong fifteen-year marriage told us: "Of course we fight. Our marriage is worth fighting for."

Conflict Is a Part of All Intimate Relationships

When two individuals have sustained contact with each other, conflict is inevitable. Our purpose here is not to argue the right or wrong of conflict, but rather to emphasize the fact that it affects all relationships. Think about the bickering factions in the church at Corinth (1 Cor. 3:1-4), the dispute between two women in the Philippian church (Phil. 4:2-3), the confrontation between Peter and Paul (Gal. 2:11-14), and the sharp disagreement between Paul and Barnabas that led to their alienation from each other (Acts 15:36-40).

If godly co-workers and fellow church members can't escape conflict, how can we expect a married couple to do so? In fact, when you think of all the possible reasons for disagreements, it is a miracle that couples achieve any unanimity at all. Let's look at some of the common sources of conflict.

1. *We have differing patterns of needs.* Everyone needs a certain amount of privacy and a certain amount of intimacy, but no two people are likely to require the same amount. Even if your needs are very similar, you can run into a problem of timing. A husband pinpointed the issue:

I'm fortunate. My wife and I are a lot alike in terms of how much time we need alone or with others. But even that doesn't keep us from running into problems, because we're not always on the same schedule. Just recently, I felt the need for intimacy, and wanted to hug her. She pulled away, because she was frustrated about something and needed to be alone. I got irritated, and we had a brief argument. That doesn't happen a lot, but it does happen.

Such differing patterns of needs are a frequent source of irritation and conflict in marriage. Some examples include:
• After work, he is tired and wants to relax at home, but she is restless and yearns to get out of the house.
• He likes to spend and she likes to save, and each is uneasy about the other's use of money.
• She craves for someone to listen, but he seeks a time of quiet.
• She wants to spend time with her parents, but he desires time just with her.
The list can be expanded indefinitely. Yet the point should be clear. We are not talking about "right" and "wrong," but about differing perceptions of "what I need at this time." Both spouses' needs at a particular time may be legitimate and appropriate. But they may also contradict each other, and this can lead to conflict.

2. *We live with many sources of stress.* Stress challenges our capacity to relate in a Christian way. Stress makes it more difficult to be patient, kind, and sensitive to the needs of your partner. Stress, in other words, puts a strain on your relationships as well as on your personal well-being. The loss of a job or the threat of job loss, problems at work, serious illness of a family member, death of a loved one, and problems with children are some of the stressful events that can strain marriage. Even the incessant barrage of news about crime and violence can depress us, make us fearful, and thereby impede our ability to maintain a vibrant marital relationship.

A father told about a problem with his child that strained his marriage:

Our son got caught up in drugs in high school. We needed to work together to help him. But at first, we both looked for someone to blame for the problem. And I'm sorry to say that we blamed each other. That really hurt our marriage for awhile, and it kept us from helping our son.

Stressful times can make a marriage stronger, of course. But stress is always a challenge. Whenever you are stressed out by work or a family situation or something that is happening in your life, take special care to guard your marriage. Make your spouse your ally in your struggle with the stressful situation.

3. *We develop new perspectives.* Because something is a problem now does not mean it will always be so. On the other hand, because something is not a problem now is no guarantee it will never be a problem. We all develop new perspectives—on what we need, what we want, where we want to go in life, and so forth—and those new ideas and attitudes can be a source of marital conflict.

Joe and Evelyn were married twenty years when they discovered how new perspectives can bring turmoil into marriage. Evelyn was a housewife for the first twenty years of their marriage. She and Joe had agreed that he would be the breadwinner and she would take care of the home. From time to time, she had an itch to do something more, especially after all the children were grown and gone.

Evelyn's itch intensified as she watched some of her friends go back to school or take on part-time or full-time work. The first time she raised the issue with Joe, he told her there was no need for her to work because his income was sufficient for their needs. The second time she raised it, he was more heated in his reply and pointed out that he needed her at home to prepare his meals and keep the house in order for him to concentrate on his work. She responded that she needed to do something more than that. He reminded her that they had agreed he would be the breadwinner. She said that decision was not one of God's commandments, written in stone, and that after twenty years she needed something more in her life. He stormed out of the house.

Joe's resistance only made Evelyn more determined. One morning she announced that she intended to look through the want ads and pursue the possibility of some kind of work. Joe became not only angry but caustic: "No one will want you. You're not trained to do anything other than what you're doing right now."

Evelyn persisted and found a job as a receptionist in a physician's office. She assured Joe that she would continue to take care of the house and prepare his meals. Their arguments continued for a time. But then, we are pleased to report, Joe's perspective also changed:

> I fought her all the way. But you know I finally realized that going to work made Evelyn so happy and so excited that I had to accept the fact it was good for her. When I did that, I found it was also good for our marriage. She has grown as a person. She is more engaged with life and more fun to be with now. Our marriage is better than ever.

Not every case of conflict over new perspectives has such a happy ending. For if the new perspective of one spouse results in conflict, it may be necessary for the other spouse also to develop a new perspective in order to resolve the conflict. That doesn't always happen. When it does, the marriage is enriched.

4. *Men and women are different kinds of creatures.* Recall that men and women tend to communicate differently, and that can result in conflict. A researcher asked nearly six hundred people to tell exactly what someone of the opposite sex did that led to conflict, and found some similarities but also some differences. Men complained about sexual rejection, about the moodiness of women, and about women spending too much time fretting about their appearance and too much money on their clothes. Women complained about sexual coercion and exploitation, about being treated in demeaning ways just because they are women, about men's failure to share feelings, and about men's tendency to be insensitive and thoughtless.

The point is that, while men and women have some of the same needs and values and standards, they also have some that differ. The differences may be rooted in culture rather than biology, but they still cause considerable conflict. In our society, for example, men feel a need to be in control of situations, while women feel a need to facilitate good relationships. Note how this can result in conflict in a situation where a husband commits himself and his wife to social activities with his colleagues at work:

She: You're always making plans without consulting me. (She is offended with his behavior because discussing plans is a way to maintain the intimacy of a relationship.)

He: I can't wait to talk it over with you every time I have to make a decision about something. (He is offended because for him to check with her means that he isn't in control of the situation.)

She: But you're making decisions for me as well as for yourself. (She is angered even more because he misses the point that this is a relational matter.)

He: It can't be helped. Somebody has to do it, and we can't wait until we have time for a conference. (He is angered even more because she doesn't understand how he would look to his colleagues if he told them he had to check with his wife before making a decision.)

Such arguments can go on endlessly without either spouse ever being fully aware of the roots of the conflict. On the one hand, such conflict can damage your marriage. However, if dealt with appropriately, it can also help your marriage and enhance the overall quality of your relationship. Let's see how.

Conflict Can Help Your Marriage

Knowing that conflict can benefit your marriage won't make you enjoy the conflict, but it will save you from the illusion that conflict is a sign your marriage has failed. To be sure, too much conflict can be ruinous to a marital relationship as well as damaging to children. But a moderate amount of conflict can help your marriage in a least five ways.

1. Conflict can save a marriage from dry rot. People who never fight may not be involved sufficiently with each other to have an intimate relationship. Conflict, by contrast, is a refusal to let a relationship deteriorate into death from the dry rot of indifference. Because most of us do not like interpersonal conflict, you may be tempted to avoid it. Keep in mind that the result may not be the peace you had hoped for, but an emotional divorce from your spouse.

Perhaps you have an image of marriages breaking apart under a hail of verbal bullets. It is important to note that some marriages end with a whimper rather than a bang. They are slain not by warriors, but by the slow, silent erosion of intimacy. A woman whose fifteen-year marriage ended this way told her story with sadness:

> We never fought. But we never talked much either. And when we did talk, we never talked about the things that were happening to us or that were bothering us. And one day we decided on divorce. We didn't talk about why either one of us wanted the divorce, or about what went wrong. We just split.

By the time they agreed on a legal divorce, they had already divorced emotionally. Some honest arguments might have saved their marriage. In conflict, you are emotionally engaged with someone else. In conflict that is managed well, your emotional involvement will lead to heightened levels of intimacy.

2. *Conflict brings issues into the open.* Few things are more frustrating than to have someone angry with you for a reason that he or she won't tell. Joe and Evelyn, who had numerous arguments over her desire to work outside the home, had some days when they didn't argue—days that Evelyn called "maddening":

> We *should* have been arguing. Joe was angry. I knew it, but he wouldn't tell me why he was mad. One day, we were at the shopping center, and when we came out I just plopped down on the trunk of the car and told him I wasn't moving until he told me what was wrong.

Evelyn had started working when the incident occurred. Joe's anger, she discovered, arose from the fact that she had been late with their dinner on a couple of occasions. He saw that as proof that she could not deliver on her promise that their home life would not be disrupted by her job. "He tends to pout," she said, "and would have been that way for days if I hadn't insisted he tell me what was wrong."

When Joe finally told her why he was angry, they had an intense argument. But that was good. The argument brought the issue out into the open and enabled them to deal with it. They clearly could not deal with it as long as Joe was angry in silence.

3. *Conflict helps clarify issues.* When disagreements occur, each spouse thinks he or she knows what the issue is. In the course of conflict, however, each may find that the issue is somewhat different from what he or she had first thought. In the case of Joe and Evelyn, for example, Joe initially knew that the problem was Evelyn's failure to have dinner ready on time. Evelyn, however, knew that the problem was Joe's insistence that she do things the same way she always had even though she was now working.

The real issue, they discovered, was the appropriate division of labor in the home. Evelyn acknowledged that she did not hurry because she resented Joe sitting and reading while she prepared dinner. Joe admitted that it wasn't really fair for him to relax while she continued working. When each agreed that the real issue was not the behavior of either of them but how to divide up fairly the work that needed to be done, they were able to work out a schedule of responsibilities that was satisfactory to each of them.

4. *Small conflicts help defuse more serious conflict.* Molehills can become mountains. When small conflicts aren't

resolved, we tend to store up resentment for a later explosion of anger. It happened to Evelyn. Because she wanted to prove to Joe that he would not be inconvenienced, she tried not to say anything to him when he did something that irritated her. One day, she had car trouble on her way to work and was late. During the day, a patient shouted at her for something that was not her fault. On the way home, she got stuck in traffic. And then Joe greeted her with: "Where the devil have you been?" She exploded.

Actually, Joe asked the question with more concern than irritation. Evelyn overreacted. But her overreaction was the outcome of a series of frustrating incidents and weeks of avoiding any kind of disagreement. As we'll note later, some things aren't worth fighting about. But the effort to avoid all conflict is like thinking that tax deferral means tax avoidance. Sooner or later, one way or another, you have to pay.

5. *Conflict can create and maintain a sense of fairness in the relationship.* Fairness is important to marital satisfaction. Unless you feel that, on balance, you're getting about as much out of the marriage as you're putting into it, you won't feel very satisfied.

Conflict helps create and maintain the sense of fairness if you believe that the outcome enhances your well-being. The spouse who says "when we fight I always wind up feeling responsible," or "when we fight I never get what I want," does not benefit from the conflict. Each of you should feel that your own needs are met as a result of the conflict.

Joe and Evelyn both believed that they were being treated unfairly before they argued about the division of household work. The conflict, thus, enabled them to develop a course of action that made both of them feel good because each felt that the arrangement was fair. They were now working as a team again.

═══

The five benefits of conflict we have just explored are not inevitable outcomes. Obviously, some conflict is destructive. If you want your conflicts to bring benefits rather than deterioration, you need to learn how to argue productively.

RX FOR COUPLES: FOLLOW THE RULES FOR PRODUCTIVE ARGUING

1. We will allow nothing to become more important than our relationship.
2. We will not argue incessantly or needlessly.
3. We will not prolong the conflict.
4. We will strive for mutual understanding.
5. We will not attack each other.
6. We will treat our disagreement as a problem to be solved together.

Read on for more explanation.

1. We will allow nothing to become more important than our relationship. That's actually a restatement of the wedding vow—till death us do part. When we marry, we agree that we will allow no intruder to sever our relationship. Yet the intruder manages to break in and as a consequence, many marriages dissolve—over everything from power struggles (who's going to run things around here?) to money disputes (I can't live with someone who spends or saves money the way you do). A husband in a long-term, happy marriage put it this way:

We've had very few fights. We both would rather make love than war. So if a disagreement comes up, say, over something like whether we should buy some new furniture, I tell her to go ahead even though I don't feel we need it. Why should we fight over a few dollars for furniture? Sometimes I give in and sometimes she gives in. We just feel that most disagreements aren't as important as our good relationship.

We suggest that you remind yourself during conflict that whatever the issue is, it is not more important than your relationship. The goal of the conflict is to protect and enhance your relationship. Marital conflict is not a contest to be won or lost, but a process to be used for growth.

2. *We will not argue incessantly or needlessly.* Both continual bickering and conflict over trivial matters are destructive. If the issue doesn't matter that much, why fight? A lot of marital grief could be avoided if spouses would ask themselves a question before engaging in conflict: just how important is this to me?

This is the approach that Gene and Sharon adopted to salvage their conflicted marriage. Almost from the moment when they said "I do," arguments became part of their daily routine. Everything—from who should take out the garbage to who should fill up the car with gasoline—offered an opportunity to squabble.

When they came to us during the third year of their marriage, their relationship was in deep difficulty. They fought constantly, and family and friends would avoid them. Although there were some deep problems that required a significant amount of counseling to resolve, the couple did begin to work immediately on the way in which they handled conflict. One of the things that they quickly discovered was that they were fighting over things that really weren't very important. And even more revealing, they realized that arguing had become a way of life. Sharon expressed it this way:

> If Gene stated that he wanted to go out for dinner, I automatically reacted with something like, "You didn't want to go out last night when I did." And the fur began to fly!
>
> As we began to look at the things we fought about, we discovered how unimportant most of them were and determined to change our pattern of conflict. Now we try to fight about only those things which really matter.

3. We will not prolong the conflict. One way to prolong conflict is to sulk rather than to work through the issue. The noted psychiatrist, Karl Menninger, wrote about a man who went to bed and stayed there for seven years with his eyes covered because he was angry with his wife. Few people carry out their anger with such severity, but some do allow an argument to slip into a cold war of resentment because they do not resolve the issue.

When a problem is not confronted and a solution found, you can be certain that it will continue to stalk a marriage. For example, Jake and Meredith have had a running battle about her relationship with her mother since their wedding seven years ago, and they have never come up with a way to mediate their differences. The conflict nearly destroyed their marriage last year. Currently, Jake and Meredith are back together but, unfortunately, the arguments continue. They really haven't grappled with the issue that divides them. Until they do, future conflict is assured. If, like Jake and Meredith, you have recurring conflict over some issue, you may need a better technique of dealing with it. The sixth rule of productive arguing can help.

The happiest couples we know insist on following the biblical principle: "Be angry but do not sin; do not let the sun go down on your anger" (Eph. 4:26). As a wife happily married for nearly three decades told us: "Early on, we decided never to go to bed with unresolved conflicts. We have certainly lost a lot of sleep! Seriously, we *talk* out instead of *walk* out."

4. We will strive for mutual understanding. Think about a conflict you had with your spouse. At the time it began, what kind of outcome did you want? An apology? A promise to change? An explanation? The reversal of a decision? Any of those might be appropriate. But you won't know which, if any, are appropriate until you achieve mutual understanding. A first step in any conflict is to make sure each of you understands the other in terms of such things as: What is bothering you? What do you see as the issue? How do you feel and what do you think about this matter? What is it you want to see happen or not happen?

Some arguments, like some communication generally, are two monologues interrupting each other. A productive argument is one in which each of you not only strives to get your point across, but also works at understanding the other's point. You can reach that point of mutual understanding more quickly if you employ the simple technique of role reversal. In role reversal you stop pressing your own points, and each of you expresses the position of the other to his or her satisfaction.

Role reversal helps clarify the issue for both of you. For instance, a couple argues about money. He accuses her of spending too much, of being a "budget-buster." She accuses him of being a tightwad, and argues that she has a perfect right to spend what she wants since she contributes half of the income. There seems to be no solution. Frustrated, she says: "Let's make sure we understand each other. You tell me how I feel about this."

His first attempt is: "You feel like you should be able to spend any amount of money on anything you want." She rejects that and has him try again. He expresses her position to her satisfaction when he says: "You feel like you're providing half of our income and that you should be in on the decision as to how much we spend and how much we save."

Then she tries to express his point of view. He is satisfied with: "You are worried about our financial future, and think it's important for us to save a particular amount of money each month."

They now understand each other. In the process, each has seen the reasonableness of the other. They are ready to work together on a resolution that is acceptable to both of them.

5. *We will not attack each other.* Intimacy offers us the opportunity for enhanced well-being. It also makes us vulnerable. No one knows better how to hurt you than someone with whom you are intimate. In the heat of argument, it may be tempting to pull out all the weapons and attack your spouse. You know where your spouse is the most defenseless. You know what will hurt the most. You have a powerful weapon. Resist the temptation to use it. As a happily married husband advises: "Bite your tongue and never say anything to your spouse that might linger or persist. If you want to inflict hurt, you can with words. Angry words persist."

You are more likely to attack your spouse if you approach conflict with the attitude: "You are a problem." A productive way to approach conflict is: "We have a problem." When you approach it that way, you are ready to make use of the sixth rule.

6. *We will treat our disagreement as a problem to be solved together.* The problem-solving approach means that the focus of the struggle is no longer you versus your spouse, but rather you and your spouse versus a challenging or

threatening issue. You may, of course, still argue over the best way to deal with the issue. But the emphasis is not on who's going to win; instead, it's on how we're going to deal with this difficulty.

In the problem-solving approach, you begin by coming to agreement on what the problem is. Keep in mind that the problem is *not* your spouse. The problem may be the way your spouse behaves. But even if that's true, it often can be framed in a productive way. A couple having conflict over housecleaning was still in the "you are a problem" mode. He said the problem was that she was a messy housekeeper. She said the problem was that he was a perfectionist. The counselor said: "Neither one of those is the real problem. The real problem is, how do you get the house cleaned in a way that's acceptable to both of you?" Their disagreement took a productive turn when they changed the way they identified the problem.

Once you agree on the problem, try to come up with as many ways to resolve it as you can. Don't evaluate the ways at this point. Just make the list as long as you can. Among other things, the couple with the housecleaning issue came up with: I can keep things in better order, but probably not as good as you want (her); I can live with somewhat lower standards, but probably not as low as you would prefer (him); we could get some outside help; we can each be more careful about making a mess in the first place; we can eat out more so we don't mess the kitchen; we can alternate which one has the responsibility for cleaning.

Creating alternatives changes the conflict from "your way versus my way" to "various ways that might work for us." When you have exhausted your creative energies on this part of the process, discuss which of the alternatives you will try. You may want to use one or a number of them. Try one. If it doesn't work, then try another until you find a satisfactory solution.

Because they were both working, the couple with the housecleaning dispute opted for an outside cleaning service. He resisted it initially on the grounds that "I'm not an upper-class person who has servants." He finally realized that he would be more comfortable with the service and a more orderly house than he would with the other options and a somewhat messier house.

The problem-solving approach is useful for dealing with any kind of issue. It doesn't mean there won't be anger or some heated discussions. However, it is a wonderfully productive way to deal with conflict. Use it, along with the other rules of productive arguing, and your conflicts will nourish your marriage.

EXERCISING PRODUCTIVE CONFLICT

Do the following as a couple or in a group with other couples:

1. Which of the six rules of productive conflict do you violate most often? Discuss what you can do to follow the rules.
2. Practice role reversal by using it to discuss an issue about which you disagree.
3. Recall a recent argument or two. Discuss how you would have handled it differently by using the problem-solving approach (Rule #6).
4. Brainstorm ways to avoid attacking each other during conflict. Keep a list of those that you believe will be useful to you and review as needed.

8

Change

I am making all things new.
—Revelation 21:5

CHANGE CHECKUP

Answer each of the following questions, then read on to see how change affects the health of your marriage.

1. In a good marriage, you don't try to change each other, you accept each other for what you are. True or false?
2. What are your spouse's annoying habits?
3. In what ways would you like your spouse to be different?
4. What change in your marriage would make you feel more intimate with your spouse?
5. What do you think your spouse would like to change about you?

ome people argue that you must learn to accept your spouse as he or she is, for trying to change your spouse only threatens the marriage. We believe, however, there are some things you help your partner change and some you accept. The trick is learning which is which. We'll discuss this later.

First, let's get a perspective on this notion of change and see how it can nourish your marriage.

We All Change

The supposedly romantic notion of "stay just the way you are" doesn't square well with the fact that we belong to a God who is "making all things new" (Rev. 21:5). In fact, to say to your spouse "you've changed, you're not the person I married" can be a cause for celebration rather than lament. For if variety is the spice of life, then being married to a changing person is an adventure that enhances the quality of life—*if* the person is changing in a desirable way, of course.

The point is that every marriage is a relationship between two changing people. Everything, from the cells in our bodies to at least some of our attitudes, beliefs, and behavior patterns, changes over the course of our lives. The challenge is to change in a way that increases rather than diminishes your intimacy.

If one of you changes in a way that is incompatible with the other, your marriage will be troubled. When Dennis and Karen were married, they took great delight in the fact that they were both lawyers and even planned for the day when they could open a legal practice together. Five years later, however, Dennis is restless:

I hate the confinement of working in a large downtown firm and, more importantly, I really don't like being a lawyer. So much of the work that I do seems so petty. I know I really don't want to do this for the rest of my working life. What I really want is to open a nursery on property that we own on the outskirts of the city! I studied horticulture as an undergraduate and have stayed active in the field as an amateur gardener. I just know I can make a go of it. But when I told Karen that I wanted to leave the firm, she exploded. She said that she had married a lawyer, and wouldn't settle for anything less. We are currently at an impasse.

For Karen, the fact that Dennis is not the man she married is a source of pain.

On the other hand, many people agree that their spouse is not the person they married, but they find that a cause for rejoicing. For example, Brad and Julie are both professionals, both pursuing different careers than they planned on when they married. Brad talked about his seventeen-year marriage as a shared adventure in growth. He said that he and Julie "are more deeply in love; our friendship grows as we affirm each other's growth. . . . We grow more satisfied each day. Growth is what our marriage and our lives feed on." And another husband said that the changes he and his wife experienced kept bringing them to new levels of heightened satisfaction with their marriage.

Change, then, can either threaten or nourish your marriage. The trick, as we have noted, is to control the changes in your lives so that they increase your intimacy.

You Need to Take Charge of Change

Some changes, of course, are beyond your control. For example, you may lose your job because of the economy. Job loss is likely to be a challenge to your marital intimacy because it tends to be so stressful. You can control your reaction to the change, but you can't control the change itself.

On the other hand, there are many changes that you can control. In particular, there are three kinds of changes that you can control in order to grow more compatible:

1. You can reduce the number of annoyances in your relationship.
2. You can add intimacy-building patterns to your marriage.
3. You can make changes in activities, attitudes, values, and beliefs a mutual rather than a unilateral affair.

1. Reduce the number of annoyances in your relationship. Asked what she had learned since her marriage a year earlier, a wife said: "I've learned just how many things my husband does that are really annoying." She said this half-jokingly, but also half-seriously. She had learned what we all eventually learn about our spouses—they can be fairly irritating individuals at times. How often have you heard or made such complaints as:

• "He doesn't pick up after himself."
• "She writes checks when we don't have enough money in the bank to cover them."
• "He always interrupts me when I'm telling a story to someone."
• "She's always late."
• "He never does things when I first ask him."
• "She spends too much time talking on the phone with her friends."

It's these annoying kinds of behavior that bring "marriages made in heaven" crashing back to earth. Well, keep them in perspective. After all, every intimate relationship—from friendship to marriage—involves annoyances. Think about the ways your parents, your children, your friends, or your co-workers have all irked you at one time or another. Face it, any two or more people in sustained contact will find each other irritating on occasion, even the married couple that seems to be the "perfect" match and have the "perfect" relationship.

For marriage, then, the point is neither to find someone who will never annoy you (you won't) nor to work on your spouse until all the annoyances are gone (you can't). Rather, the point is twofold. First, keep the annoyances in perspective. That means not only recognizing that annoyances are inevitable in an intimate relationship, but also keeping in mind that annoyances are a two-way street. Your spouse irritates you in some ways, but you also irritate your spouse.

Second, work to reduce the number of annoyances in your relationship. Try this: for your next anniversary, or Valentine's Day, or just a day of marital enhancement, agree to give each other a special gift of one annoyance removal. Each of you tell the other one thing he or she does that annoys, or one thing he or she fails to do that annoys, and then work together to remove those two annoyances. You still won't have an annoyance-free marriage, but you will have a better one.

2. *Add intimacy-building patterns to your marriage.* Within a year after getting married, couples tend to change in two ways. First, each tends to do more things that displease the other, such as not doing something that your spouse asked you to do, criticizing your spouse, or complaining about something your spouse does or does not do. This was the problem we addressed when we suggested you reduce the number of annoyances in your relationship.

Second, each tends to do fewer things that please the other. Typically, spouses spend less time approving or complimenting each other, saying something to make the other laugh, saying "I love you," and sharing feelings, thoughts, and problems with the other. This is the problem we address when we suggest you add intimacy-building patterns.

What builds intimacy? Shared activities. Mutual self-disclosure. Expressions of affection and admiration. Expressions of caring and thoughtfulness. If you have gotten so caught up in work or child rearing or other activities that you have little or no time for nurturing your relationship with your spouse, it's time to change and add some intimacy-building patterns to your life.

Every marriage needs ongoing nurture. The nurturing may take the form of something elaborate like a weekend away. But there are also simple and easy ways to nurture your marriage. Brad and Julie admitted that they sometimes feel distant from each other because each is in a demanding professional career. Whenever the feeling occurs, they take action to restore what Julie calls their "connectedness" with each other:

> From time to time I realize that I don't feel very close to Brad. It's like there's some kind of gap between us that I don't like. How do I bridge that gap? Sometimes all it takes is to just talk together. We talk about the news or about our work or our family. It doesn't have to be profound. The important thing is that we are connecting to each other and affirming our oneness.

3. *Make change a mutual rather than a unilateral affair.* We noted that the marriage of Dennis and Karen is in some turmoil over the issue of his changing professions. Dennis's desires have changed, but Karen's have not. Such unilateral changes are a frequent source of marital problems.

Dennis made a mistake in the way he handled his changing feelings. Certain that Karen would not be pleased with the way he was feeling about being a lawyer, he decided to avoid a confrontation and said nothing to her for several months. Only when the need became intense did he broach the topic with her, and then he bluntly announced that he planned to leave his firm and start a nursery business. The announcement quickly led to the first in a series of arguments.

A better approach would have been for Dennis to have shared his changing feelings when they first began. Early on, for instance, he might have said to Karen: "I really feel that I have made a wrong career choice. I've been practicing law for six years, and each year I like it less. I know I need to make a change." Dennis may not have avoided arguments with this approach, but think about some of the possible outcomes if he had shared his changing feelings with Karen all along. Karen would have had more time to reflect on Dennis's needs and would have felt a part of helping him decide how to meet them. They might have used the problem-solving approach we discussed in the last chapter and come up with various alternatives that he could try. And in the end, they might have arrived at the same conclusion—that Dennis leave his law firm and open a nursery.

In other words, as you sense your own perspective changing, talk about it with your spouse. You may bring your spouse along with you, or you may modify the direction in which you have started to go. Whatever the outcome, the goal is to guide the change so that you and your spouse are more rather than less compatible.

What, and How Much, Do You Change?

Recall that you don't have to live with *any* and *every* irritating thing your spouse does, and your spouse does not have to accept all of your irksome ways. So how do you know what to change and what to accept?

Let's begin with something you will need to accept—fundamental personality traits. At least, you will need to accept them for the most part. For instance, an introvert frequently marries an extrovert. There is nothing perverse or sinful about being either. But extroverts sometimes try to get their introverted spouses to become more "out-going." Bill is a highly introverted engineer who attends, with his wife, a young married couple's group. At their social functions, Bill typically sits quietly and listens to others. On the assumption that Bill wasn't enjoying himself, his wife and some of the other couples tried a number of times to engage Bill in conversation and to get him to mix more. Finally, he told them: "I really enjoy these get-togethers. But I won't if I have to act like the rest of you."

Bill's wife initially found it annoying that she had to "carry the responsibility of being sociable" at the parties. She would still prefer him to be more outgoing. But, for the most part, she has learned to accept him for what he is—an introvert.

What then do we mean to accept such traits "for the most part"? Introversion and extroversion, like all personality traits, vary. You are not "either-or," but "more of " or "less of." And you can modify your behavior. Bill will never be an outgoing extrovert. However, he can exert some effort and mingle a bit more at parties. To do so will certainly make his wife more comfortable and will also allow others to get to know him.

As this suggests, there are two questions to be answered when we think about changing some of our spouse's annoying behaviors: which ones do you try to change and how much should you change them? Is his introversion one of the things that Bill can modify? Yes. How much? Only a little and only on certain occasions.

Some things, of course, may need to change completely. If your spouse, for example, has the habit of driving the car until the tank is completely empty, it won't be enough just to reduce the number of times he or she is stranded on the highway in a given month. The only acceptable change is to break the annoying habit completely.

Keeping in mind, then, that we all can and do learn to live with some of the annoying habits of our spouses, how do you decide which ones need to be changed, and how much they need to be changed? There are two steps to be taken, each of which involves a cost-benefit analysis. You do the first step alone, and the second with your spouse. For each step, you address the same three questions. In the first step you use these questions to decide whether a particular annoyance is one you will learn to live with or want changed. If you want it changed, you proceed to the second step and use the three questions with your spouse to get consensus between you.

The first question is: *What are the costs of accepting the behavior?* Break these down into personal costs (such as irritation and extra work), interpersonal costs (how it affects the way we feel about each other and about living together), and costs to the spouse with the annoying behavior (does this in some way degrade or detract from the spouse?).

For example, after ten years of marriage Betty decided that it was time to confront her husband, Stan, about his annoying habit of never hanging up his clothes and letting them fall wherever he took them off. "I knew it wasn't something sinful," she said. "So I had to decide if I had the right to confront him, especially since he had been doing it for ten years without me saying anything. But since I have started teaching again, I just don't have the time or the energy to pick up after him, and our bedroom is a disgrace." Betty thought about the costs of accepting Stan's habit. She couldn't say that it degraded or detracted from him as a person. But it certainly added irritation and extra work to her life. And it made her feel that he wasn't thoughtful of her needs and didn't care about their home. Fortunately, she was wise enough to recognize that the situation, if permitted to continue, would eventually erode their relationship.

Counting the cost, Betty decided she should definitely confront Stan. But there is a second question: *What are the benefits of changing?* The benefits to Betty were obvious. What about the benefits to Stan? Again, we can think of them in personal, interpersonal, and spousal terms. From a personal point of view, she decided, he would think of hanging up his clothes as additional work. Her gain might be his loss! Still, there were benefits. He would know that he was helping her. He would feel good because she felt better and more appreciated. And perhaps he might even feel better about himself because he had done something that both enhanced their relationship and facilitated the household work. Again, the analysis indicated to her that it was appropriate to raise the issue.

The third question is: *What are the costs of changing?* Even if it costs something to accept the behavior and there are benefits to changing, you may not want to proceed if the costs of changing are too great. For instance, if Bill's wife had been determined to make him into an extrovert, she would have found the costs far too high. Among other things, most likely she would have alienated him in the course of trying to achieve an impossible task.

In the case of Stan and Betty, however, the costs of changing did not seem to be as high as the costs of not changing. It would cost Stan some additional effort. It would require Betty to be patient and to remind him when he reverted back to the old habit. On balance, then, this appeared to Betty to be an annoyance that should be eliminated.

At this point, when you have answered thoroughly each of the questions for yourself, you have a number of options. You may decide that the costs of trying to change the behavior outweigh the benefits, and that this will be one of the annoyances that you give your spouse. "Personally, I don't like cats," a husband told us. "And I don't like the time my wife gives to taking care of our cats. But I also know it would hurt her deeply to give them up. So I try to find other things to do while she does her thing with the cats." He had decided that the costs of getting rid of the annoyance far outweighed the benefits.

Your second option is simply to tell your spouse how the behavior affects you and offer to help change the behavior. Note the "offer to help." *Anything you want to change in your marriage is a mutual responsibility.* It isn't a matter of "this is your annoying habit so please change it." It is, rather, "let's work together to change the behavior that is troublesome to me so our relationship will benefit." If your spouse agrees, decide how you can help with the change.

If your spouse doesn't agree, or no change occurs in spite of agreement, work together through the three questions. Perhaps your spouse is reacting to a cost or a benefit that you haven't thought about. Or perhaps your spouse disagrees with some assumption that you have made. Stan, for example, initially resisted Betty's idea on the grounds that "I'm too tired when I come in from work to hang up my clothes. Besides I'm either going to throw them in the laundry, take them to the cleaners, or wear them again. So what's the problem?" Betty pointed out that for years she had picked up after him but that now her teaching schedule just didn't leave her with enough time. She also reminded Stan that she had always maintained their bedroom as a special place—their place to escape from the many responsibilities in their lives and to be together. It mattered, therefore, how it looked. Stan acknowledged that all she said was true and agreed to change.

━━

All change is a mutual responsibility. Even if, for example, you and your spouse both agree that one of you has an annoying habit that must be changed, you both have some responsibility for bringing that change about. The following principles are useful for any of the three kinds of changes we have discussed.

RX FOR COUPLES: HELP EACH OTHER CHANGE

1. Be encouraging and supportive while being firm.
2. Model the behavior you would like to see in your spouse.
3. Use rewards.
4. Make change a shared adventure.

Read on for more explanation.

1. Be encouraging and supportive while being firm. In other words, be gentle with each other. As Paul advised the Galatians, "If anyone is detected in a transgression, you who have received the Spirit should restore such a one in a spirit of gentleness" (Gal. 6:1). Gentleness is not weakness. It is, rather, the absence of such counterproductive approaches as trying to berate or bully or shame your spouse into changing.

For example, Brad is confident and successful in all he does, but he was not always that way. He told us that earlier in his life he had many self-doubts and often complained to Julie about his fear of failure and his inadequacies. One day, Julie startled him when she said that she admired men who were strong and self-confident and that she herself needed a husband like that.

She said it in a way that made it sound like a request, not a put-down. She told me that she thought I was very competent and very strong, but that I needed to act more that way. I determined from that day on that no matter how I felt in a situation, I would try to appear strong and self-confident. I did, and I have become that kind of person.

2. *Model the behavior you would like to see in your spouse.* Would you like your spouse to compliment you more often? Would you like more displays of affection? One place to begin is with your own behavior—do more of those things yourself. Be a model. As Jesus told us: "In everything do to others as you would have them do to you; for this is the law and the prophets" (Matt. 7:12).

To put it in negative terms, you can't expect your spouse to behave in a way that you do not. At this point you may agree that you shouldn't expect your spouse to behave in ways that you don't, but you may still question whether modeling the desired behavior will lead your spouse to change. The answer is, sometimes.

Take the intimacy-building behaviors we began with, more compliments and displays of affection. Put your spouse to the test by increasing such behaviors yourself for a few weeks. You're likely to see your spouse reciprocate. And you'll both probably feel closer to each other.

Sometimes the modeling needs to be combined with verbal encouragement. Mike and Denise told us how they were dealing with a problem that is common—one partner (in this case, Mike) has trouble sharing feelings. Mike is learning because Denise both models the way for him and frequently encourages him to try to articulate what he is feeling. Both the encouragement and the modeling are crucial, as Mike pointed out:

I'm introverted, so I don't talk easily about a lot of things, including my feelings. I also haven't had much practice, because my family doesn't do it. And I guess I also feel that, as a man, I should always be in control, so I really have a hard time talking about negative feelings. But Denise won't let me be quiet. She can tell by looking at me when something is bothering me, and she insists that I talk about it. It's tough, but I'm learning. And it really helps me to see her doing it. If she tells me how she feels about something first, it's easier for me then to tell her.

Although it can be very effective, modeling won't work for everything. You may, for instance, be fastidious about picking up your clothes and find it has no effect on your messy spouse, or scrupulously careful about keeping records of your checking account and find your spouse continuing to be careless. When modeling doesn't do the trick, even modeling combined with verbal encouragement, you may need to use the cost-benefit analysis we discussed. If so, be sure to use a system of rewards once you initiate the effort to change.

3. *Use rewards.* A wife told us that the "most annoying" thing her husband does is to get angry with her but say nothing. In discussing it, we discovered that when he did try to express his anger, she would sometimes say "You shouldn't feel that way." In effect, she was punishing him for doing what she said she wanted him to do! "Even if you think his anger is unjustified," we suggested, "let him know that you appreciate the fact that he expressed it. Then talk about why he is angry and what the two of you can do about it."

As the example suggests, rewards are not necessarily something tangible like money or gifts. Appreciation and encouragement are powerful forms of reward, and they should be used freely. If, for instance, a husband agrees to change his irritating habit of procrastinating, his wife should compliment him each time she asks for help and he responds without her having to repeat the request. She might object: Why should I reward him for doing something he should have been doing all along?

Think about the way God relates to us. From the very beginning, God has promised rewards to those who pursue right ways: "Now therefore, if you obey my voice and keep my covenant, you shall be my treasured possession out of all the peoples" (Exod. 19:5). In a sense, we could say that obeying God and keeping the covenant is what we should be doing anyway, so why should God reward us?

So even if your spouse is only doing what he or she "should have been doing all along," resist the temptation to think in such terms. Be godly. Offer some gratitude and praise. Rewards are a powerful tool that spouses can use to help each other change. When you use rewards, you are working as a team. You are no longer your spouse's watch-dog; you are a helpmate.

4. *Make change a shared adventure.* We have already discussed one way to make change a shared adventure—whenever you feel yourself changing, bring your spouse in on it so that you can guide and experience it together. Another way to make change a shared adventure is to initiate some changes. Remember that change can add vitality to a relationship, particularly when both spouses like the change. You are both more apt to like it if you have planned it together.

What kind of change can you initiate? Here are two examples:

• Do either of you feel that any part of your life is in a rut, or has become so routine as to be a ho-hum experience?

If so, find a way to change it. You may want to change your schedule (when you shop, or when you have sexual relations), your division of labor in the home (let her take care of the outside and let him take care of the inside of the house), your weekend activities (do we always have to go to your parent's house for Sunday dinner?), and so on.

• Periodically talk about your hopes and dreams for the future. Where would you like to be in your marriage, your faith, your work, and so on, in the next year or the next five years? What dream vacation would you like to have someday? What would you like to be or to do if you could have your ideal? Some of your hopes and dreams should be realizable. Start working together to make them happen.

When you do such things, you will find change to be your ally rather than your adversary. It will nourish your relationship. Instead of yearning for a way to keep things just the way they are, you will look forward with anticipation to the next surprise around the corner.

EXERCISING CHANGE

Do the following as a couple or in a group with other couples:

1. Each of you offer to change something that is annoying to the other. Develop a specific plan for making the change.
2. Make a list of twenty or more ways you can reward each other. Save for frequent reference and use.
3. For the next two weeks, reward everything your spouse does that pleases you.

9

Community

Bear one another's burdens.
—Galatians 6:2

COMMUNITY CHECKUP

Answer each of the following questions, then read on to see how community affects the health of your marriage.

1. What role do other people play in your marriage?
2. How many of your friends have strong marriages?
3. To what extent do you share your marital challenges and struggles with other people?
4. If your marriage was in trouble, with whom would you be willing to discuss the matter?
5. To what extent are your in-laws a help rather than a problem?

*A*n old song says that Molly and me and baby comprise a "blue heaven" in which all of us will be happy. It doesn't work that way. No family, like no individual, is an island. Families, just as individuals, need the support of others in order to stay healthy.

Therefore, community—all those people who are part of your marital support system—is one of the crucial resources for a lasting and satisfying marriage. It is a preventative against the malady of trying to go it alone. It may sound romantic to say to your spouse "You're my everything," but as we noted in chapter 2, no one can possibly fulfill all the needs of his or her spouse. To attempt to do so places an intolerable burden upon both individuals and upon their relationship.

Let's look at some other reasons why community is important. Then we'll explore ways you can strengthen your community ties.

You Need Others

Both you as an individual and you as a couple need others. To be an integral part of a community adds glue to your marital relationship. The stabilizing effect of community is well illustrated by the fact that couples who move to new locations where they are strangers are more vulnerable to breakup.

Richard and Allyson barely survived such a move. They now fully appreciate the importance of community. Several years ago, they and their two children moved across the country after Richard took a new job. Their marriage had been a good one. They had been part of a group of couples in their church and lived near Allyson's family. But they knew no one in the West Coast city where they moved and delayed starting to church in the busyness of getting settled into a new home.

Their problems began when Richard spent increasing hours at work in order to establish himself firmly in his new career, and Allyson spent increasing hours trying to get the house in shape, getting the children settled in school, and also looking for employment of her own. They found themselves becoming strangers to each other. The time they did spend together frequently was marred by one or both being irritable and argumentative. Each began to have thoughts of ending their marriage.

Thankfully, they started going to a church that had a support group for married couples. There they found people who talked quite openly and frankly about various issues and challenges of marriage. They were able to talk about the problems with which they were struggling and discovered that other couples in the group had been through similar experiences. How reassuring to know that their problems were not unique! The group also encouraged them to start dealing realistically with their situation and helped them get back on track with their marriage.

Richard and Allyson know well the meaning of community as a crucial resource for marriage. Allyson is not sure her marriage would have survived without the community they found in the group: "I would have come to church the first Sunday after our move if I had known how much help we were going to need."

Some couples seem to sense their need for others from the beginning. We were touched by a wedding service that included, near the end, a part in which the couple, Cathy and Al, called on those present to be a part of their marriage. After the exchange of vows, the minister told the congregation that this was a special event for Cathy and Al. They had made their covenant with each other to live the remainder of their lives together. And now they wanted those gathered to support and affirm that decision. The minister, in accord with the couple's request, posed a number of questions to the congregation and asked for their response:

Will you commit yourselves to provide all of the encouragement and support possible to help Cathy and Al in their marriage? If so, please answer "I will."

And do you agree to do all in your power to assist Cathy and Al in the struggles that they are sure to encounter as they strive to build a Christian marriage? If so, please answer "I do."

And will you yourselves strive to live out lives of commitment, so that Cathy and Al may see in you that toward which they too should strive? If so, please answer "I will."

Aware of their need for community, Cathy and Al determined from the outset to enlist the aid of friends and family to help them in their quest for a lasting and satisfying marriage.

You Need Others for Support

One of the things Cathy and Al asked for was support. It was a wise request. There are a number of kinds of support that we all can use from others.

1. *You can use support for difficult decisions.* Our lives are a never-ending series of decisions. Each day you make decisions about such things as what to wear, what to eat, which of your endless chores to attend to, what TV programs to watch, and so on. And even seemingly simple decisions can be difficult. Have you ever had an argument with your spouse, for instance, that began merely as a discussion about whether to buy a new piece of furniture, or how to discipline a child, or if you should spend Saturday afternoon at your in-laws?

Some decisions are even more difficult than others, for they can affect the whole course of our lives and the quality

121

of our marriages. Examples of the kind of decisions that are both difficult and likely to have serious consequences for our lives include deciding to:

- have a child or a second or third one;
- start a new career or change careers;
- invest in a home;
- bring aging parents into your home or place them in a retirement home;
- use an experimental medical procedure for a critically ill loved one;
- confess to your spouse something you have done that he or she will regard as betrayal.

Your support group can help you with such decisions by talking through them with you, offering their insights and perspectives, and helping you to clarify your own feelings. For example, a couple struggling with whether to continue supporting an adult son who had problems holding a job, discussed the matter with another couple in their church. They didn't want to alienate their son, but neither did they want him to continue to depend upon them to bail him out every time he got into financial difficulties. They found the insights of the other couple invaluable:

> They had some experience with this in their own family. They helped us see that we couldn't take any risk-free course of action. And they introduced us to the notion of "tough love." As a result, we have let our son know the limits of what we will do for him. And we have begun to see some positive results. We really appreciate our Christian friends.

Helping us see the appropriateness or rightness of various alternatives is an important way that others support us in the decision-making process. A couple who wrestled with the issue of what to do with aging parents discussed their options with friends. They had considered a retirement home, an apartment with some outside help, and bringing their parents into their home. The parents were open to any of the options, but the couple felt guilty about not bringing them into their own home. Christian friends who felt that either a retirement home or an apartment of their own would be a preferable arrangement gave the couple the support they needed to make their decision. Today the parents are happily living in an apartment complex for senior citizens and enjoying their independence.

2. You can use support during times of the marital blahs. We've asked hundreds of couples to draw a chart for us of their marital satisfaction over time. They all note fluctuations, times when marital satisfaction has been high and times when it has been low. During the low moments— those times of the marital blahs—the support of family and friends is essential.

Some people find the necessary support in a group of couples in their church. They learn that everyone goes through such times and realize that it doesn't signal the end of romance and vitality. Some find the support in friends and family who sympathize with their discomfort and encourage them to work through the low time. Some find the support in a marriage encounter weekend that offers ways to rebuild your intimacy. The point is, there is a lot of support to help you get through the marital blahs, and you may need to use that support to bring your marriage back on track and keep it growing.

3. You can use support for dealing with annoyances and problems of everyday living, and for making changes that enrich your relationship. We've discussed ways that you and your spouse can work together to minimize annoyances. At times, you may need the support of others to deal effectively with those annoyances, with various problems of everyday living, and for making enriching kinds of changes.

Let's say that you, your spouse, or both want to do something that will enhance the quality of your relationship—stop a habit like smoking, or make a personal change like losing weight, or alter a stressful lifestyle such as being committed to too many activities. Letting others know what you have decided to do will increase your chances of success. People who announce that they are going to stop smoking, for instance, will be encouraged and monitored and, should they relapse, reproved by those who heard the announcement.

In other words, rather than making annoyances or problems or changes a personal or marital task, make them a community effort. A couple who wanted to deepen their spiritual lives, both for personal and marital reasons, made a number of attempts but kept falling short of what they hoped to achieve. They decided to enlist the help of other couples in their church. Now they are part of a group of Christians who meet regularly and help one another to grow spiritually.

4. *You can use support in times of crisis.* To be in a crisis is painful. To be alone in a crisis can be devastating. "Bear one another's burdens" (Gal. 6:2) is good psychology as well as good theology. No burden is ever quite as heavy when someone else is sharing it with you.

Both your personal and your marital well-being can be either damaged or strengthened as you work through a crisis. The death of a child, for example, is one of the most severe crises any couple can face. Many marriages do not survive it. The spouse may be a continual reminder of the loss or, perhaps, the partners blame each other to some

124

extent. Whatever the reason, marital breakup often follows the death of a child. But we have seen marriages that did not break up, because the couples were embraced and supported by family and fellow Christians in a community of shared grief and hope.

A crisis, then, is no time for some kind of macho bravado. It is no time for a "this is something *I* have to cope with" or even "this is something my spouse and I have to deal with." Crisis is a time to call on the community, that we may fulfill our calling to bear one another's burdens.

You Need Others for Guidance

Others can guide us in two important ways. First, we can take advantage of their insights. Sometimes others can see a solution that eludes those who are struggling with a problem. Phil and Nancy had a problem that is common—they disagreed about how their income should be spent. Phil was more of a spender, and Nancy was more of a saver. Each thought the other dealt unwisely with money.

"He'll see something he really likes, and put it on the credit card and bring it home," she complained. "The other day he bought $1,000 worth of computer equipment that we don't really need."

"She is always worrying about the future," Phil responded. "I know we need to save, too, but we also need to live *now.*"

Phil and Nancy each approached the issue from the standpoint of trying to get the other to change an erroneous view. They made no progress until they attended a marriage enrichment group. The leader devoted a session to money problems. He pointed out that disagreement about how to allocate family income is a common marital problem. Then he asked the group, "Do you each have a written budget that you agree on?"

Phil and Nancy were one of a number of couples who did not. The leader pointed out that a budget can resolve a lot of the kind of arguments that begin with, "Why did you buy . . . ?" If the partners have agreed to the budget, then any purchase that falls within budget guidelines should cause no problem.

The leader made another suggestion: If possible, include a discretionary item for each spouse in the budget. That is, each spouse should have a specified amount of money that can be spent, saved for future spending, or put into a savings account. "The money is yours to use as you please, no questions asked," the leader said.

Phil and Nancy took advantage of the insights. "We still have an occasional disagreement," Nancy admits, "but the budget and the discretionary funds have just about wiped out our problems."

The second way others guide is by their behavior. Parents are the first guides to married life that individuals encounter. In fact, unless you consciously decide to do otherwise, you are likely to relate to your spouse the way your parents related to each other. This may be good for some kinds of behavior, but it is not always the best way. Even if your parents' ways were good for them, not all of them are necessarily right for you. And some of them may be detrimental. A wife told us that she was working on the way she handled conflict with her husband:

> My immediate tendency is to try to win quickly by coming on loud and strong. I know I do that because that's the way my father argued with my mother. It worked for him. It wasn't so good for my mother. And I don't want to do that with my husband. But it's a

struggle. Every time we argue, I have to watch myself and remind myself not to do that.

Because there are characteristics that are common to good marriages, you can benefit by observing the good marriages and using them as guides. Perhaps your parents did things for each other that can enrich your marriage. Perhaps some friends have practices that you can adopt to your marital profit. For an interesting and potentially useful time, ask a couple who have the kind of relationship you want to tell you why their marriage appears to be so vital and meaningful. They'll probably be delighted to talk about it, and you may pick up some ideas that can enrich your own marriage.

You may think that community is unlike the other marriage resources we have discussed, in the sense that you have less control over it. It depends, after all, not just on you and your spouse, but on the reaction of other people. Nevertheless, there are a number of ways in which you can strengthen your community.

RX FOR COUPLES: STRENGTHEN YOUR COMMUNITY

1. Nurture family relationships.
2. Maintain a group of friendships.
3. Get to know other people who are committed to their marriages.

Read on for more explanation.

1. Nurture family relationships. Parents, siblings, and other relatives can be an important part of your community. Even if they do not live in your area, you can maintain contact through the telephone and mail. The healthier your relationships with your family, the more you and your marriage will benefit.

In-laws can be particularly important. When you are close to your in-laws, they are likely to support the marriage and not just your spouse during times of difficulty. A wife whose marriage was in peril for a time told us that her sister-in-law helped her immeasurably:

> She understood my position, and stood by me. She wanted my marriage to succeed, but she didn't blame me for the troubles. In fact, she even went with me when I consulted with a lawyer about the possibility of divorce. I know it sounds odd, but she's part of the reason my marriage didn't break up. I needed someone to understand my point of view, and she did.

Incidentally, in-laws have an undeservedly bad reputation. Stories and stand-up comedians, among others, have portrayed in-laws in a way that is unrealistic. Most people have good relationships with their in-laws. Some even find a second family, like the husband who told us that his father-in-law had become the father he never had (his father died when he was an infant).

2. Maintain a group of friendships. The healthiest people, and the healthiest marriages, are part of a group of friends. Friends can provide the support and guidance we all require. Although you can only maintain a limited number of friendships at any one time, always be on the lookout for new ones. This is particularly vital in today's mobile society when people come and go in our lives.

Making new friends may be painful because of the difficulty in finding couples with whom you are compatible. Like Mel and Sandy, two successful professionals, you may find yourself getting on well with one partner but not as well with the other. Mel and Sandy have a strong, twenty-two-year marriage. But they know the need for friendships to nurture their marriage. As Mel put it:

Any experience is richer when you share it with someone else. If I see a great movie, I am thrilled. If Sandy sees it with me, it makes it doubly enjoyable. And if we go with another couple, we have yet another layer of enjoyment added to the experience.

Mel and Sandy have moved a number of times as they have pursued their careers. Sandy noted both the way they cultivate new friendships and the problems they have encountered:

We usually start with work or church. We talk about the people we meet and decide on someone to invite to our house for an informal dinner. Sometimes it doesn't work out well. Mel once had a colleague he thought he would like to know better. It turned out that we both really liked his wife. But as we got to know them better, we found that he and Mel really had nothing in common except their work. We stayed friends, but it wasn't as satisfying as some other friendships we've had.

Mel and Sandy knew something else. Like many people, they made the assumption when they first moved into a new area that everyone else was already firmly locked in a network of friendships. "And some people are," Mel pointed out. "But we eventually realized that a lot of people, even some who have lived in an area for many years, are really anxious for, and open to, new friends."

3. Get to know other people who are committed to their marriages. The more you associate with people who are committed to marriage, the greater the benefit to your own marriage. New friends, for example, need to be compatible in terms of interests, but also in terms of commitment to marriage. Mel is in his second marriage. He and his first wife were involved with a number of other couples who stressed "having a good time." His first wife left him and married one of their friends, who also had left his wife. In Mel's second marriage, he and his wife got involved with a couples group at their church. They have become close friends with two of the couples and spend most of their leisure hours with them. "Everyone in this group is working to have a good and lasting marriage," Mel said. "We have a good time, but we also spend time helping one another make our marriages stronger."

How do you find other couples committed to marriage? As with Mel, church is one source. To be sure, Christians also struggle with marital breakup. But the church still stands for and supports marriage for life. Many churches have marriage support groups or couples groups.

A number of organizations and activities exist in most communities that support marriage. The Association for Couples in Marriage Enrichment has chapters throughout the United States, many of which conduct seminars and workshops. Denominational-sponsored marriage encounter or marriage enrichment weekends can be found in all large communities. Marriage and family therapists in cities frequently present classes or workshops.

Even if you don't begin a new friendship or maintain contact with people you meet at a class or weekend gathering, you will benefit from the guidance you receive as well as the awareness that a lot of people are like you—anxious to make their marriages last a lifetime. As someone has said, marriages may be made in heaven, but they have to be lived out on earth. And it helps to be around other people who are committed to making their heaven-made marriages work on earth.

EXERCISING COMMUNITY

Do the following as a couple or in a group with other couples:

1. Ask some happily married couples you know what makes their marriages strong and fulfilling. Adapt some of their ideas to strengthen your own marriage.
2. Invite a couple who seem to have a strong marriage to your home for dinner.
3. Write a note of appreciation to a family member who has made a positive contribution to your marriage.
4. Join a group that supports marriage.
5. Attend a marriage enrichment weekend.

10

*C*hrist

For I have set you an example, that you also should do as I have done to you. —John 13:15

FAITH CHECKUP

Answer each of the following questions, then read on to see how faith affects the health of your marriage.

1. How does being a Christian make a difference in your marriage?
2. How often do you bring the resources of faith to your marriage?
3. How does being a part of a church strengthen your marriage?
4. In what ways could you and your spouse share more spiritual experiences?
5. How can you use your faith in Christ to deal with the challenges and difficulties in your marriage?

fter five years of marriage, a husband said that no part of his life was the same. His marriage, he said firmly, had transformed his life:

I feel better about myself in many ways. I feel better about my relationships with others. I feel better about myself, about my health and physical condition, and about the way I use my recreation and leisure time. I do more living now than I have ever done before. In this profound sharing, I feel that I have grown as a person and as a human being.

Clearly, he rejoiced in his marriage. That's the aim of all the marriage resources we have discussed—to create marriages whose dominant theme is joyous sharing. We have chosen to discuss Christ last, not because he is less important than the others, but precisely because we regard him as central to a lasting and healthy marriage. We want you to end your journey through this discussion of marital enrichment with your thoughts focused on Christ.

But first, we need to be realistic. We know that Christian marriages can also fail. We know, too, that some people without faith have a lasting, healthy, and satisfying marriage. Nevertheless, the importance of Christ to marriage is underscored by the work of researchers at the University of Minnesota. In their study of 6,267 married couples, they found that the great majority of those with the richest marriages have a shared faith, which they believe brings meaning and strength to their relationship. Those in the best marriages are likely to agree that their love for each other and the love of God are intertwined. In other words, bringing Christ into your marriage raises the odds that you will achieve what you hoped for on your wedding day. Let us, then, explore the specific ways in which Christ nourishes marriage.

Christ Enriches You Personally

If you are committed to Jesus, you have entered a new dimension of life. You are his creation. As you continue to be nurtured, shaped, and enriched by his working within you, you are increasingly anchored in peace and hope. You greet the morning with anticipation and walk through the day in confidence. You are able to relate in love and to leave others with a touch of the divine in their lives. You put no limits on the good that can happen, because you know that the same power that spoke the world into being and that raised Jesus from the dead is the power that is at work within you. At times you grieve and groan and struggle and stumble, but eventually you find yourself again in the embrace of his love. In short, Jesus adds immeasurable richness to your life. And that, in turn, makes you a better marriage partner.

The point is, anything or anyone that makes your life more meaningful and satisfying also enhances the quality of your relating. People who are difficult to get along with are generally struggling with themselves and with the meaning of their lives. They have poor interpersonal relationships because they are not at peace with themselves or with the circumstances of their lives. People who are anchored in a fundamentally gratifying life, on the other hand, are apt to have good relationships. Christ anchors them to a meaningful life. In doing so, he also enriches the quality of their marital relations.

When Greg and Ellen were first married, he was not a Christian. Within a year, a serious problem developed. Greg found other women attractive to an extent that was not only obvious but also hinted of future infidelity. "I could see the lust in his eyes," Ellen said, "when we would be with a group of other couples or when he was talking to a good-looking woman." Ellen, who was a committed Christian, responded to the situation by praying regularly for Greg and for their marriage.

After a particularly irritating incident, Ellen asked Greg about his feelings. She told him that it really hurt her when she could see how much he wanted another woman. In an effort to mollify her, Greg promised to start going to church with Ellen. He also became a little more careful when Ellen was with him, but he clearly was still attracted to other women.

As long as he had to be in church, Greg decided to try to understand the service and what the Christian faith was all about. After some months, he became a Christian and a member of the church. He soon joined Ellen in praying for God to release him from lust. They are now working together on the problem, and Greg is making progress. "If I find myself getting too turned on by a woman at work, for instance, I just call home and tell Ellen about it and ask her to pray for me. That works."

Greg also has gained some understanding about the root of his problem. "I love Ellen, but I didn't want to miss out on anything. I desperately wanted to, as they say, get all the gusto from life. And with Jesus, I finally have."

Christ Models the Way

Although never married, Christ models the way for husbands and wives in an important way—he shows us how to relate to others. Jesus not only taught, but practiced in his own life, such things as doing to others what you would like to have them do to you, loving others as you love yourself, forgiving readily and without limit, and showing understanding and compassion for those who are struggling and hurting. Such qualities are the stuff of which the most gratifying marriages are made.

Jesus also called his disciples his friends (John 15:14-15). We have studied hundreds of couples in long-term marriages. One of the most important ingredients of a long-term, happy marriage is to have a partner you like, admire, and enjoy being with. In other words, the happiest and most stable marriages are those in which the spouses regard each other as best friends and enjoy being together.

Here is a husband's testimony to his Christ-committed wife:

> She is my lover, my companion, my partner in faith, and the best friend I have. I would rather be with her and do things with her than with anyone else I know. She expects a lot out of me, but never more than she is willing to give. She is always there for me. She lets me know when I fall short, but she also makes me feel good about myself and about life.

Clearly, his wife does for him many of the same kinds of things that Jesus did for the disciples. And his wife says that he does the same for her. By following the model of Christ in relating to each other, they have fashioned a marriage that sounds like it is made to last.

A Shared Faith Deepens Your Intimacy

Think about it this way. Couple A are very different. He likes work, the stock market, quiet evenings at home, and chess. She likes play, the movies, going out to eat, and roller skating. Couple B, on the other hand, are alike in many ways. They both like music, hiking, and eating out, and they share the same political views. Which couple has the deepest intimacy? Which one has the most exciting marriage? Actually, couple A divorced after five years of a conflicted relationship. Couple B have been married for twenty-three years, and according to the husband: "I thought that growing older would mean less excitement in our marriage, but in many ways it is more exciting than ever. And we feel closer to each other than ever before. Our marriage isn't getting old or stale, it's getting better."

The two couples illustrate a point we made earlier: the more things you have in common with your spouse, the more intimate you will be. Now carry that a step farther. If something like preferring the same kind of leisure activities can enhance your intimacy, what is the impact of sharing the same faith? It is the difference between having something at the periphery of your lives in common—like two circles that touch each other at a point in their circumferences—and having the core of your lives in common—like those same two circles overlapping because their centers are at the same point. A shared faith in Jesus Christ deepens your intimacy in a way that other things cannot.

Scott and Sherri, who have been married for twenty-one years, agree on the central importance of faith. As Scott said:

I think a strong and healthy relationship with God that is shared by the mate is vital. It has helped me in feeling and believing that God somehow directed our lives together and daily supports and sustains our marriage. Marriage is a journey into life with a special person as a companion. The challenge is to grow together and avoid that which weakens this goal.

Scott told us some specific ways in which a shared faith has helped him and Sherri "grow together" over the years. For one thing, their Christian faith shapes their perspectives on various moral and political issues. "We have some friends who constantly argue about male-female issues," he said. "We don't do that, because we go at those issues from the point of view of our faith."

Another way in which their faith enables them to grow together is their understanding of the purpose of their lives. "We each believe that we are here for God's purpose," Scott noted, "and that our marriage is a part of God's plans for our lives. We're working together to find and follow his plans."

Finally, their shared faith means that they regularly come together into the presence of God, an experience that gives special meaning to their relationship. "When you have worshiped together," Scott pointed out, "and prayed together at meals, you feel a special bond with each other. We're more than married. We're married *in Christ*."

———

In Jesus, the book of Hebrews reminds Christians, you have a high priest whom you can approach boldly and "receive mercy and find grace to help in time of need" (Heb. 4:16). The invitation is for marital as well as personal times of need. And the offer of "grace to help" is one that most of us will need frequently, because we live in an era of multiple strains on the bonds of marriage.

The strains range all the way from the unrealistic expectations we discussed in chapter 2 to the sheer number of people around us who have experienced a broken marriage. When a great many people are divorced or divorcing, the process may seem to be a more acceptable way to deal with a troubled relationship. In fact, you may even find people encouraging you to break up your marriage if you are in a time of dissatisfaction.

We counseled a man whose wife threatened to file for divorce. One day he told us that a divorced friend of his wife's had advised her not to delay: "If you're unhappy in your marriage, you better get out of it as fast as you can." The friend's advice intensified the wife's fears that she might waste time trying to rebuild a marriage that would never be satisfying again to her.

With so many such forces tending to pull people apart, what kinds of "grace to help" are available to add glue to relationships? Actually, more resources may exist than you realize.

RX FOR COUPLES: USE THE SPECIAL RESOURCES OF A SHARED FAITH

1. Use the Bible for guidance and encouragement.
2. Use prayer to strengthen bonds and help rebuild intimacy.
3. Regularly engage in active worship together.
4. Practice the fruit of the Spirit and ready forgiveness.
5. Tap into resurrection power to change directions.

Read on for more explanation.

1. Use the Bible for guidance and encouragement. The Bible equips Christians "for every good work" (2 Tim. 3:17), and one of the good works is building a lasting and satisfying marriage. A husband of fifteen years told us how the Bible helps him and his wife in their marriage:

We have many problems in life, but we have always helped each other through the power of God's words and we have come through many storms. Somehow the Scriptures are what give us strength, and we say this by experience and not just lip service.

The Bible is not a "quick fix" for every problem you encounter. The point is, rather, that various Scriptures can give you both encouragement as you struggle with problems and guidance on how you as a Christian can resolve those problems.

An effective way to tap this resource is to develop a set of biblical passages that will be your marital guide and comfort. One way to do this is to use a daily devotional guide together. In addition to the comments of the guide, discuss ways in which each passage you read might be a help in your marriage. In a booklet, write down passages that strike you as particularly helpful, and refer to them frequently as reminders of what God is doing and what you each need to do in order to build a lasting and fulfilling marriage.

2. *Use prayer to strengthen bonds and help rebuild intimacy.* "Love your enemies," Jesus taught us, "and pray for those who persecute you" (Matt. 5:44). Why pray for them? So that they shall stop persecuting you? No. To pray for your enemy is one way to love your enemy. To pray for your enemy keeps you from the corrosion of hatred for your enemy. When you pray for your enemy, in other words, you begin to change your feelings toward your enemy. Indeed, you can't pray for anyone, friend or enemy, without feeling more positive toward that person.

Use prayer regularly to intensify your positive feelings toward your spouse. Pray for your spouse's well-being, for God's guidance and care for your spouse, for your spouse's growth in grace and knowledge of Jesus Christ. And when the bonds of your marriage are strained, continue to pray for your spouse and for your marriage. Prayer helps to rebuild the intimacy, and is a continual reminder that yours is a God-called and God-empowered relationship.

3. *Regularly engage in active worship together.* By "active worship" we mean that you do more than just attend services—sitting and listening and then resuming your normal routine as though you had not worshiped. Talk together about the worship experience. What moved you? What did you learn? Was anything said or sung that could be applied to your relationship? Just sharing your experience of worship with each other, like all sharing, enhances your intimacy. Sharing your experience and exploring the spiritual lessons to be learned and applied to your relationship enhances an intimacy grounded in Christ.

4. *Practice the fruit of the Spirit and ready forgiveness.* What will happen in a marriage when each spouse is striving to practice "love, joy, peace, patience, kindness, generosity, faithfulness, gentleness, and self-control"? (Gal. 5:22). Clearly, it would be an adventure of growing intimacy and fulfillment.

We suggest that you use the fruit of the Spirit to enrich your marriage by working on each of the qualities in the following way. Set aside some time to discuss one of the qualities. You can begin with love, and work your way through, or you can select one that you feel would be of particular value to cultivate for your relationship. Each of you respond to these questions: What does this mean for a marital relationship? What would the behavior of husband and wife look like if each were practicing this? In what specific ways can each of us put this quality into practice in our marriage? How can we help each other develop and sustain those specific ways we have identified?

Please note the word *specific.* If you're talking about love, for example, don't come up with something too general, like "I need to show more affection." Instead, be specific, like: "I'm going to show more affection by kissing you at least once every day, and by calling you at work at least once each week to tell you I love you."

Don't wait until you think you have perfected one quality to start on another. But don't move too quickly, either. When to move on to another should be a joint decision. And you should periodically review how each of you feel you are still doing on those on which you previously worked. The point, of course, is not merely to talk about the fruit of the Spirit, but to incorporate that fruit into your marital relationship in very practical and visible ways.

Of course, no matter how hard we try to live out these principles, we will fail at times. As God graciously forgives us, be ready graciously to forgive your spouse for failures. For this project—indeed, for all your efforts—you should agree that you will each practice the forgiveness that Jesus commanded. Ready forgiveness does not mean that you take your responsibilities less seriously. Quite the contrary. It means that you are determined to build the best possible marriage and that you will not allow some of those inevitable failures to sabotage your quest. The one who asks for forgiveness obviously regrets the failure. The one who grants forgiveness encourages renewed effort.

5. *Tap into resurrection power to change directions.* Never underestimate your capacity to change directions when your marriage is not working as well as you would like. After all, "the Spirit of him who raised Jesus from the dead dwells in you" (Rom. 8:11). And God, by the power at work within us "is able to accomplish abundantly far more than all we can ask or imagine" (Eph. 3:20).

It is a mind-boggling point. The power that raised Jesus from the dead is the same power that is at work within us.

With such power available, you are never helpless or hopeless. Neither is your marriage.

Charles and Kayla had been married seven years when they reached a low point. For about two years, their marriage had been in a kind of downward spiral. Charles found himself increasingly disappointed and irritated by Kayla's lack of organization in caring for the house and their three small children. Kayla found herself increasingly frustrated and angered by Charles's "perfectionism" and unwillingness to assume any responsibility around the house. Their arguments were frequent and often intense.

At their low point, neither was strongly considering the possibility of divorce. But each hoped for little more than a "let's do what we can to live in peace." Neither expected to recapture the excitement and intimacy of their earlier years. For neither thought the other would change much.

In spite of their mutual pessimism, Charles and Kayla have radically shifted directions in their relationship. They are rebuilding and at times experiencing a taste of the delight they found in each other in past years. How have they done it?

First, they each agreed that their Christian commitment was to lifelong marriage. They agreed to not consider divorce, but to focus on how they could construct a meaningful marriage. Second, they acknowledged that, as Christians, they had the power available to alter the course of their relationship. Third, they worked with their counselor to understand better each other's position. Fourth, at the counselor's suggestion they developed specific ways that they could change their relationship, including ways to incorporate the fruit of the Spirit into their marriage.

Charles is now helping Kayla with the home and children. Kayla is working on being more organized and orderly. They are setting aside one night a week for a "date." They are each trying to be more patient with the other, recognizing that change is usually fitful rather than smooth. They are each trying to find specific ways to affirm their love for each other. In essence, they are using their God-endowed power to change themselves and the course of their marriage.

EXERCISING FAITH

Do the following as a couple or in a group with other couples:

1. Holding hands, pray aloud for each other and for your marriage.
2. Read 1 Corinthians 13 together, then discuss how you can apply the qualities of love to your marriage.
3. Try to find something in each worship service you attend that will benefit your marriage.
4. Volunteer to work together in some project sponsored by your church.